The Shadow of The Truth's Heart

By Eric C. Bonner

First Printing

www.amazon.com

All Poetry original works by Eric Christopher Bonner

Send all inquiries to:

Emanwarrior@gmail.com

http://Facebook.com/Emanwarrior516/

Table of Contents

Shadows of The Truths Heart

Maybe you could understand if you can close your eyes and see an old slave crying for freedom/

Not only can I see him, I feel his pain in my slumber/

Same faith in God trying to hit a number/

The inequity of the sin I swim in is not abnormal/

I come to the dance dressed formal/

Fully knowing my testimony is far from normal/

That these verses are touched by an angel that drowned his sorrows in gin/

Voices yell from the pits/

"God is gonna tell you something right now"/

While the nation is split in two/

And the fires are burning and Hebrew brothers and sisters are still being killed/

The chess board is full of pawns/

The cross still burns on certain people's lawns/

The bible is for sale/

The degree earned comes at a price/

Carnal desires burning with disease/

Open thy eyes and God forgives is getting hard to believe/

The pain we walk with is hard to relieve/

When the slain are slaughtered for pennies/

And you're praying for a save/

While the government is praying you stay a good slave/

"Faith without works is dead"/

We break bread with our Judas/

The devil knew us the same way Jesus grew us/

The dreamer dies alone/

The evil die wanting to hurt more/

The content die with a smile/

The hurt die by their own devices/

The cost of success varies in prices/

The soul is sold off more than you know/

The tears flood heaven's gate/

And hell can't wait for more souls to torture/

The bullets are engraved for both saved and unsaved/

Even a demon can hold up a Bible and hurt protestors/

Children are abandoned by the curbside/

The disease and enemy has always been us/

The evil has never been ghosts but flesh/

The problem is the justification of evil/

Even when it's see through/

When the noose still hangs in republican and democratic windows/

And the smell of murdered negroes on American soil is felt when the wind blows/

When we did more to put food on the table than any other body that was able/

Slept next to the horses in the stable/

Then killed our brothers like Cain did Abel/

Selah, Allah Akbar/

We have travelled far with a foot on our backs/

The tracks lay over the weak/

No inheritance for the meek/

But we all dream of a mill/

Still waters run deep/

And I have visions of my past joys in my sleep/

But I know that they are just – SHADOWS OF THE

TRUTH'S HEART!

FOREWORD

This book is in honor of all those souls that perished from Covid-19 alone with only the whispers of death in their lungs. May you gain the peace in the afterlife that this world did not provide for you. In honor of one Harvey White who died alone in his apartment, just another soul from the south who chased his dreams in New York City in the 50's/60's and failed. Rest easy.

"We are all hurting, and we have to, no we must heal. We have to stop hurting each other because hurt people only hurt other people" – Eric Christopher Bonner

To those that have hurt me, I forgive you! I only wish I was a better Uncle, Husband, Father and son.

God Bless you all who purchased this book.

PART I -

President

President

In the middle of NYC, you will find a stoop that raised me/

No praise please, I was forced to run for office due to the

lack of knowledge my opposition possesses/

At the top of the poetry game I guess being the best makes

me restless/

My guest list only contains God/

Odd but few can hold a lighter to my candles flame/

My aim is straight I never waste a bullet/

Any enemy you send me is dead before the trigger gets

pulled/

"Put another shrimp on the Barbie"/

Rest in peace to Harvey/

My lyrics are hearty/

Partly because the stew I brew contains more truth than most can chew/

The blue skies hover above/

I pack a full clip of love/

In the middle of hell floating on a pissy mattress/

Writing my sonnets daily, "that's practice"/

Facts is when I am at this little to nothing matters/

The towers fall/

A plane lands in the Hudson/

"It was all a dream", I used to read the source magazine/

Dreamed of the mics my lyrics could score/

I just know that I wanted to be known in poetry for more than being –PRESIDENT!

THE SHADOW OF ME

Sun shines brightly/

The echoes of my pain frighten me/

The fire that rages in my soul enlighten me/

Trying to find the right in me amongst so many wrongs/

The songs sung in A minor/

The keys to my soul naked for the world to see/

Trying to find the rest of me in the mess of me/

Searching for destiny amongst the best of me/

Digging through the deserted rubble for what is left of me/

Praying that God forgives me, yet gives me peace and
redemption/

Dying each day in poverty's wisdom/

The rhythm of my blues in melancholy shoes/

I paid my dues when my mother's death became news/

Traversing this land of red, white and blue/

Knowing that the blood of my poetry is an auto biopic of

the enigma of E/

Gazing at the blue sky wishing to be-

Greater than the SHADOW OF ME!

ME

Really/

I'm far from a legend/

More frail and insecure than any hero in a tale/

I lied and told you I was more/

Just a man with a broken core/

An old thief, I stole from the corner store/

Not a criminal by any means/

I am just a product of an environment where love is a
mystery/

I ran my mouth because that is all I was blessed with/

I worked to be smart/

But being smart does not dictate what fate will bring/

When those who hug you disappear into empty seats/

The heart beats and breaks in sync/

It really does not matter what I think/

My soul dies on the brink of madness/

In the ghetto on a pissy mattress jumps the spirit of me/

Before life hit me/

And I longed for the world to get me/

On the stoop in the city heat, quarter water in hand/

Sits a wide hazel eyed kid with a smile that goes on for a mile/

Dreaming to be better than the future version of - ME!

BRIGHT

The moon illuminates the darkness/

The kiss upon my lips soft yet subtle/

The oils massaged in tenderly/

A volcano still in the twilight/

An explosion of passion glazes the sheets/

The beating of the heart sped up by fingertips/

The motion slow yet steady/

The soul left drifting in the air/

Lost in a place where ecstasy slides underneath moans of

pleasure/

Where the tongue gets hidden in places where the hands are

lost/

Trying to taste the essence contained in you/

And the cost is too much to bear/

Where the throbbing subsides with unbridled sensitivity/

And the breathing is strained/

The skin is stained with passion/

Where each crevice is explored and defeated/

The kisses seated with intent to destroy/

The shaking of legs and the search to be held/

While the world stops on a dime/

The moist remains of treasure tasted lovingly/

The darkness of life lifted if only for a moment/

The light shines on sweaty sheets/

And the moon shines this night - BRIGHT!

STAGE

I paint the walls with my blood/

The tapestry was sewn in my tomb/

The room was aglow in my sorrow/

Lost in time, none left to borrow/

The lyrics hid my tears/

My anger suppressed my fears/

The sky illuminated blue/

The lies spread falsely, so many friends mixed them with what was true/

Lost in the nights watch, nothing left to do/

Cept count the seconds, minutes and days/

I know now that my life is unfair/

A whodunnit tinged with who, what and where/

My dreams, a bowl shattered amongst the concrete/

In a world now where you miss the intimacy of touch/

My words are lost in the twilight zone because no one can

read hieroglyphics painted with care/

They just film your demise then laugh with no disguise/

God should have killed us a long time ago/

Before Ike beat Tina/

Before love lost to lust/

Before heartache opened the door to mistrust/

Before we stopped loving and started killing us/

Before the last seal opened and the signs from revelations

all sprang true/

I close my eyes to dream and all I ever see is the end/

Perils around every bend/

I walk in the blizzard of life toting a Bible/

While the preacher rides first class/

And he looks at me and shakes his head/

Cause my ribbons in the sky fly tattered and torn/

Cause every single thing I held tightly, left me like the air

from a choke/

My tears fall in the darkness/

My heart breaks in the day light/

My hope dies in the mirror/

My passion dwindles with age/

But my faith is a roaring river and a flood that opens

heaven's door even on the hardest - STAGE!

LAND

I often ask myself do you know what depression is?/

Is it that in my moments of joy I feel sorrow?/

Is it the tears inside my soul because I long to not see
tomorrow?/

Is it the idea that because I have gained success that you
don't see the mess of me?/

If I showed you my scars would you think less of me?/

So even if I feel blessed to be me, I still feel the hurt of my
yesterday/

It talks to me in my restless sleep yelling "I won't go
away"/

All I do is joke, smile and pray all day/

But inside I am lost looking for a way to save me/

Looking for a mother who never saw me graduate junior high or college/

Living the best that I can trying to pay homage/

My knowledge was learned at end of a gun while my father was robbed/

That is my life summed up in one stanza/

Bullets in the chamber that could have saved me a long time ago/

No black fist pick in a Afro in Macy's Brooklyn/

No truth to tell about a legend or friend/

No broken heart to mend/

No pain, no gain, no joy and glory/

No born again, then again there is no story to tell so well/

Just the vision of what was in the stars/

Galaxies colliding over Mars/

No love turned to hate/

No debate on how great the poetry was or how to rate a
rebel's lines on a confederate flag/

No dude in Brooklyn with a NASCAR jacket rapping
Rakim's lines to Eric B for president/

And "that's cool because I don't get upset, I kick a hole in
the speaker pull the plug and then I jet"/

My love ran away like Luda trying to release therapy/

No argument with your best friend a week before the streets
killed him/

Not enough time to make up/

That is why I don't sleep now because I'm trying to wake
up/

Even if I have my apron on trying to cake up/

Even when jealous ones still envy/

And the spirit of Jose or Jimito lives in me/

I am strapped to the good of the hood/

Even when there is a bat in my hand/

I am just soldier of God at the end of the day searching for

a peaceful place to - LAND!

1350

For the ghosts of 1350/

Your laughter still echoes down the halls/

In the backdrop of gin and drug wars/

Bullets crash my window/

A little boy on all fours/

Leaking ceilings and paint peeling/

The feeling of cold air when there is no heat/

There is no gas, so a hot plate is your date/

Or there is no electricity so you're borrowing light with an extension cord/

Or a can of beans is all that you can afford/

Praying to the Lord for relief from a por mans grief/

I had to work like Kunta to bite successes apple/

Had to be willing to cut a throat killing for freedom/

Le Amistad sunken with the blood of my masters/

But, 1350 survived many disasters/

Broken sewage lines and sanitation fines/

Dreams scattered over a Christmas light decorated second

floor balcony/

I was bound to be a light in utter darkness/

This is my omega tinged with Nintendo, PlayStation and

Sega/

I controlled what I could/

The casket bare, splintered wood/

Shielding my bones from the rain, I dwelled inside a

hurricane/

Names like Coffee, JC, Teddy, Corine, Cora, Clyde,

Juanita, Ronette, Mary, Dennis, and Gramby dance in a

ghostly trance/

The poker table lay empty/

The laughter gone/

The quiet encapsulates the atmosphere/

Gone are the southern voices that escaped Jim Crow/

Gone-/

Colored only signs/

Strange fruit hung from pines/

Separate lines and hatred filled eyes/

The pain travels too/

The lead paint covers you/

 Sub-par education stains the residue/

The skies forever blue/

The love far and few/

But in the middle of our turmoil we can always look back

on you – 1350!

PART II -

Message

Message

Stars love to bug when I ski/

My degree of wisdom comes from falling and never busting a shot/

I fell down and caught a literal knot/

On the block I watched a little me get jumped while the police laughed/

So, excuse me when my automatic burst nightly/

I leave the scene unsightly/

Seal the shells up tightly/

I fight for those walking the path in the hood like me/

I am rightly the king of poetry/

Wakanda forever, brother and sisters/

Rest easy Chadwick, the ancestors welcome you/

Uplifted a whole race, made a whole case that we are super human/

No room in this hall for black on black crime/

Peace king with a peace ring/

I'm feasting on each line in my notepad/

A master MC gave me hope when none was had/

Just a kid on the IRT/

Probably be a statistic was realistic/

But I know I can be what I want to be was the melody/

Took a trip to QB when I was a young prodigy/

Chasing a love probably meant to disarm me/

But I formed more hope and developed my Chi to where impossible is nothing like Ali/

I am the greatest wordsmith from my part of town/

Blood from Rosewood all over my gown/

Paint over my tears like a lost clown/

The whole town is laughing at me probably/

On my Pendergrass blue notes ring in hand/

Sifting the sands of time in Persia/

I am the best left out and I said it with my chest out/

In the heat I happened to spoil/

In the field of cotton and moonshine I toil/

Under fire I never boil/

God wrapped me with foil/

Even when I was blinded, I could see what I was destined
to be/

Then when I looked up and saw KING spelled in the
clouds/

I knew it was a – MESSAGE!

E

Sometimes the things that are dead live on/

Blood on a pillowcase/

Dreams suffocated by poverty/

Crippled by life but I did not let it hobble me/

Gunshots in my backyard, too used to it to let it bother me/

My eyes look to the stars for guidance like my
predecessors/

I looked for wisdom, but I got more of that from my life
than any professors lectures/

The scriptures tell tales of redemption/

I have walked a crooked path with a crooked laugh/

Candles of death surround my bath/

My hood has been infiltrated like the carter/

I am walking around talking about I am black and proud

playing the martyr/

I am nineties wear like starter/

I am flying a charter with a mason jar of moonshine/

I am fine unhung from the pine trees/

My steez is refined by my tears over still waters/

Now that is deep, too lyrical do not sleep/

I climbed the rough side of the mountain/

I am supposed to be in the dirt/

Yet I live through the hurt/

And every cut I still feel/

I am in my field of dreams praying for revenge/

I am binge drinking until the door falls off the hinge/

My computer degree came from a mixture of Ohms and

Kirschoffs law/

My desire came from wanting more than pain and rain/

The skirts off my reaper/

I am from the backwoods of the ghetto/

But I shine brightly/

Seen so much beauty in that hole/

Rich men never seen real joy/

We had love over those canned pork n beans/

When the money came the mirror changed/

Now we just work like a slave to keep it/

Life is too short, it is no secret/

How did we lose love when we sold our souls?/

Was it the Gucci that made us turn on each other?/

The world is in turmoil/

More taxes, the less pay didn't we gain America's

independence that way/

No party without the tea/

So, I will sit here with this Hennessy and the shadow of

what is left of - E!

WRONG

If you live long enough/

You will meet hurt/

And she lives next to despair/

Who is married to sadness but had an affair with lust/

And lust was shacking with trust/

Got married at the alter supposedly until dust to dust/

It must have been all a lie or an alibi to try a ménage à trois

/

Yeah if you live long enough you will meet pain/

And she will kill your main dish/

And leave you with sides that leave a lot to be desired/

Love been fired since our old earth retired to the heavens/

That is word to my brother Kevin/

Yet I am supposed to raise men from boys who still dream/

My nightmares scream in a bed prayed in/

In a pandemic my soul stayed in/

The devil played in the streets in elderly skin/

While the king and his men make America great/

The hate spreads like famine/

If you live long enough your own kin will turn on you like

the wind/

Then pretend you was always wrong/

Believing that treachery is invisible/

Everybody trying to outsmart the general/

Never falling in line/

They die trying to make a white line blue/

Do not let that verse go over you/

Unwilling to change is strange/

Nobody can tell you what to do/

Specially to stay inside to save your hide/

You can still catch a stray inside/

I let God decide my last ride/

I am always going stand on the right side of history/

But if you live long enough you lose track of what you did-
WRONG!

US

I sacrificed my soul for Judas/

We are all selfish, so we do us/

Kind of think if God really knew us/

He would sue us for lying about us/

We are all bleaching trying to whiten us/

Shield up to the moon trying to enlighten us/

Too many wolves out trying to frighten us/

The burden of holding my family together has been placed
upon my displaced shoulders/

My tears fall on the asphalt/

Looking around trying to find my fault line/

Indulging in the deepest wine trying to tow the line/

Knowing I gave my all so the few could ball/

Even with me draining my poetry from three/

Shooting so deep like Carolina's Curry/

Going to the hole with Lebron's level of fury/

Pleading my case pointless to a loaded jury/

Knowing that I am just a black boy like Richard Wright/

With this tone I will never be right/

Even when my essence is the light/

Screaming in the darkness of Facebook hoping you look

before the lord closes my book/

I have been more of a pawn than a rook/

Knowing that my battle can be only won by me and not -

US!

STILL HERE

A lot is on my mind today/

In the middle of another outcome of not guilty/

This skin I am wearing, it makes one feel filthy/

When really, I should be proud that we are still here/

Still here after the ships and chains/

Still here stripped of our true names/

Still here after so many rapes and planted strange fruits hanging/

Still here after being considered three fifths a man/

Still here after the cotton gin and civil war/

Still here after the marches to vote and rights just civil/

Still here after our leaders were assassinated after we assimilated/

Still here after Vietnam and the war on drugs/

Perpetuated mass incarceration and the media painting me as angry/

But America, beautiful can you see my tears underneath my scowl/

You can see that without me you are not you/

Without me, you have no rhythm and no heartbeat/

Your nothing but a country with a history of genocide on its own hide/

Can you see me girl with my flowers in hand serenading you?/

Even though you have beat and kicked me down/

It is only right that I stand on this pedestal and tell my kids/

Remember who the f - you are/

Then explain to them to respect the police that murders them senseless/

Because of a system that does not make sense/

Fear of my blackness/

Can you feel my heartbeat beating just like yours?/

Can you see me praying at night just like you?/

Even though our prayers are different it is true/

I am praying America does not shoot me or my kids in the back/

I am praying my tax money does not go to that/

I am praying you treat me better/

I am praying that I can become a light in a world filled with darkness/

I am praying you truly see me before your bullets free me from my duty on earth/

I am praying you see me than more than a black stain on your turf/

Just saying, I hope to you I am worth more/

You killed a man in front of his daughter/

This court has no order/

But one thing remains the pain I feel is - STILL HERE!

CORE

Brother Khalief Browder we miss you/

Valiant warrior of an unjust system/

You have given your life to fight for many/

They want us hunted because we have an attitude/

Locked up in the bing, only let out to batter you/

We are the most violent and the most silent/

The successful pray things get better/

The rest hope it will/

The blue or red pill Morpheus said/

Did not know both lands us on being declared dead the coroner said/

We walk a snail walk with dread to an ending with more sleep than any bed could suffer/

Brooklyn and the Bronx makes us tougher/

Bullets in the air/

Brother stretched out in his underwear/

Robbed of everything even his gear/

Where can we find peace when justice is absent/

And I am in church on Sunday praying God forgives when

American whites repent/

Sorry I do not know how to mince words/

My scriptures come from a place most high/

Most die to trying to get rich/

But I am dying to get even/

They say seeing is believing/

I am over my best friend's coffin grieving/

On the next flight leaving/

Fist in the air, sorry I do not kneel for no one, but God/

I am in the streets with fatigues on/

Fighting a war for equality with a supervisor badge on/

Headphones over my ears/

The devil herself stares at me through lustful eyes/

Visions of us intertwined in a forbidden tango/

Eating the mango in the forbidden garden/

Stirring the pot like James Harden/

Kneeling in the sea that runs red from my unarmed brother's blood/

The rosebud never bloomed for my race/

We were told by everyone even the president to stay in our place/

Our plight starts with only a trace of a ships voyage/

So, North Carolina's native son Steph Curry's invitation was revoked/

And every player was provoked to become men in the eyes

of a leader who defines them as entertainers and nothing

more/

When even God knows which dark race has built Americas

- CORE!

PLACE

Some days I doubt if I can do this/

Yeah and that is coming from a man who once slept with his version of Judas/

I exaggerated my status but knew that God had us/

So, our dreams could only grab us/

Outrunning the crooked police fully knowing they wanted to toe tag us/

The streets had us thinking of one thing because it was all about the Benjamins/

Then again, I still dream of riding my bike as I did in my youth/

Before I was the truth, my truth laid under the blue sky with the wind under my wings/

Pedaling for a quarter water/

They say the courts are out of order/

My USA got hit with racist mortar/

Can't even run for the border without being beheaded by
the cartel/

My life hasn't been roses/

I'm a victim of love and betrayal/

Blessed with wisdom and understanding/

Five percent of me drifting in the air/

Eating my bacon egg and cheese with little care/

Mother Nature hasn't been fair/

Just found out a co-worker jumped from the 21st floor/

Body hung in the air long enough for a smile to cross/

At a crossroads in life the cross should symbolize more
than loss/

Death is not a choice we should ever take in our hands/

Forbidden sands to touch/

Though many of us clutch/

Ponder while the Dutch burns slowly between our fingers/

Pain is a residue that lingers/

Young girl told me my lines made her stop being suicidal/

I told her God writes the hymn that I swim in/

He gave me the rhythm when the crimson tides were

against me/

More bama than city slicker/

In remembrance of my great Uncle Bunk I fly a last name

pridefully/

Knowing that my roots will never wither or float away in

the rain/

They will be my joy and my grace/

Until I reach my own resting - PLACE!

PART III -

When We

Cry

When We Cry

The dead cry out among the stars/

In the silence of the city lights echoes laughter and dreams lost/

The remnants of an era where crack cocaine infested us/

Where the blood of bad drug deals spill into the reservoirs/

Don't believe those who say we never wanted/

Because we wanted the world to see us/

So, the jewels twinkled in the sunlight/

And we did wrong – right/

Misled by lies and betrayals/

Many bullets emptied due to honor born from the streets/

The symphony of the bodega alarm/

The blue, white and red of emergency lights arriving with a pale horse/

Our hearts buried under the projects/

Our smiles frozen in an elementary school lunch table/

Eyes locked on a future and hands over our hearts/

Singing praises to a flag that betrayed our ancestors/

Only to grow up to be a menace II society/

And we accomplish this in a variety of ways/

Shoot our brother over a lover/

Shoot our brother over a color/

Kill over a drug deal gone bad/

Shoot aimless while innocent kids and mothers are killed/

Their bodies filled with lead/

Hate spilled on the pavement/

The tone resuscitated by those of the dead related/

We were fated to be great/

Our dreams murdered by fate/

On the surface of the moon where hate and love mate/

And we bury our Radio Raheem in the backyard/

Then pour out a little liquor because this is how it feels –

WHEN WE CRY!

MAN

I asked God why do people want to label me?/

If I'm crying, I'm depressed/

If I'm happy I'm high/

If I'm angry then I'm a psychopath/

Makes it hard to live, love and laugh/

We are fighting for existence everyday/

And you could put your life on the line for a loved one but somehow,

They don't see it that way/

And God, I want to ask them what do you see when you look at the person I'm supposed to be?/

Yet When they describe that person it seems far from me/

The tiring effect of being human in a world where our point of view can be skewed by faulty mirrors/

I fear I have lost a little hope for humanity/

No one questions the insanity of supremacy/

I know one thing, I have to start putting me ahead of the dread/

Say my prayers before bed/

Cause I know the future will be a challenge if accepted/

I'm going to keep my head on today/

Cause she is my only true possession/

Lesson is people change sometimes like the season/

And they do it for any reason/

There is no rhyme to give it justice/

So, here's my label America my name is - flawed/

Not perfect but majestic/

Not a genius, but I'm perfected/

Not Casanova, but I can hold you girl in these arms all night/

But know this, I can snore/

I can work hard to buy you diamonds out of any store/

And I raise my kids to be good God-fearing people first/

And everything else second/

I reckon I'm a little country and a little hardcore hip hop/

But the root of my family tree is planted in North Carolina and that makes me tough/

I'm not perfect kisser but you will feel my full lips on your hips/

I have a temper it's true/

But I was raised to fight for what you believe in/

And I have done plenty achieving/

All while standing over my mother's casket grieving/

All while the ghetto told me I would be nothing but a bum/

I planted my faith in God and became like Pac a rose

bloomed in concrete/

I don't know how long my buds will bring you joy/

I'm a shooting star that the heavens had to deploy/

Don't label what you don't understand/

Sit back and enjoy yourself with this incredible- MAN!

SUCCEED

Hard for me to write when the night begins to shine/

I was a teen titan with a nine/

A razor blade hidden in my Jansport/

I rolled my 4,5 and 6 in a piss filled hallways/

I beat the odds in more ways than one/

Looked up to the moon because it shined when there was
no sun/

In the darkness of my own self-pity/

I found my strength and the ability to rep a city that did shit
for me/

Except prepare me to excel in a world where the weak meet
their demise under the devils lies/

I saw my old earth fall after telling me "I'm ok"/

Those that know me say my temper was severe/

But I lived in darkness with nothing but pain there/

I birthed my flame there in virgin underwear/

Cute but labeled a threat/

Clicked up but after my homies death I claimed no set/

I walked alone like Green Day/

Cause when I got jumped while the police watched there
was no soul to run to/

2pac screamed in my head "a real man stands on his own"/

I kept myself company and we held convos alone/

Labeled a poetic genius and a loner/

People laughed when the history teacher called me boner/

There was broken glass littering the concrete/

Junkies passed out under park benches/

Somehow, I made my mark in quicksand on land unsteady/

Don't know if I'm still ready after my third seed/

Though I know one thing I'm going to jump through a

window so that each one has the chance to - SUCCEED!

STAKE

I'm prepared to be your martyr/

Tie me to the cross cause the worlds out of order/

Don't know if I can go further/

Visions of my death escape me lately/

Yet I; wonder how great I could have been with the hood tatted on me/

The depiction of me by my closest ally could paint that of an enemy/

Still I'm singing Sam Cooke "darling you send me"/

A vision of a young me under the celestial praying to be more than a cold dead body in a vestibule/

More than my momma dying a so-called vegetable/

More than Martin dreamed I could be/

We bring flowers to the dead though they smell, suffer, cry and laugh no more/

What for?

Inside a mummies tomb lays the things that brought joy to a life worrisome/

And I'm fighting so that you know God is real/

Yet more than forty bullets spilled into innocent bystanders in chi town still/

Can you find your heart mankind?/

Can you find your soul in the midst of cheating on you soulmates?/

This life takes a toll nobody knows their roll/

My police department lost control/

My president is present on the walls of hell/

Raising Cain and pain/

Bullets shattering the rain/

Families separated at the border/

A village erased by the drop or mortar/

Jesus sings the hymn in my inner ear/

He whispers save as many souls as you can "real" clear/

But those messages hold real fear when you are a young deer/

A mere mortal in the middle of my own struggles and obstacles/

He said 'E' they will follow you/

But I couldn't save my closest cousins from the dirty dozens/

I grew up in an era where mercy was a trait of the weak/

Now I turn the cheek more than most/

Dance with demons of my past and ghosts/

The host of the holy control me/

Yet they told me many years ago, my Judas would slay me/

But my demise will be the day man's eyes would wake/

So, you see there are greater things in motion and more

than steak at - STAKE!

FABLE

I been tight since 93' and you know someone who would want to try me/

Nobody in 390 would defy me/

Boys and girls high tried me/

Took it to Marcy Avenue to supply me/

Verses forged in the crack in the concrete/

The heat I spew is nothing brand new/

My brew has always been my hue with a twist of cola/

My bio folder is too hot, it will scold you/

Fire under my feet the heat I secrete has its own beat/

I made my own seat under Jim Crows residue/

I'm telling you I'm the mixture of greatness and being thrown in the pit like Joseph/

But I'm coming back for my revenge to avenge my own demise/

Surprise, the news was fake - lies/

The devil dies in my wake/

If I don't finish first, I'm last and that's shake and bake/

Open your eyes the lord cries for your boy/

Cause my brethren could spend 20 on two dime sacks/

But nothing on my book like I stole from them like a crook/

I'm on top of the Empire State Building blood spilling/

For me I see no ceiling went from a pawn to a boss/

Believe me I paid the cost/

My past crucified on the cross/

I loss more than you gained/

Trauma - when the pills got a hold on your mama/

My words pour over the canvas big as Kansas/

Man it is hot in the bitter wind chill of n y c/

I am the king of poetry/

Lo and behold thou has transgressed/

Shalt thou never wake from thou slumber/

Remember it's coming like the winter/

I'm about to hit my number with or without u brother/

I am Frankenstein's monster/

Tearing through this verse crashing my own hearse/

My heart on the table/

Don't know if I can make it to the finish line if I'm able/

But know this baby Eric Bonner wrote his own - FABLE!

CURE YOU

"This time I don't need a perfect lie/

Don't care if the critics jump in line/

I'm going to give all my secrets away"/

On a voyage that Charlie could envy/

Don't know which way the lord will send me/

Those bullets fired that hit me were friendly/

On the floor clutching my insides outside/

Wondering how I got here/

When the ceiling depicted me where the Gods sit/

I get that I was supposed to suffer where the hood died/

I never supplied the masses crack cocaine/

I left that to Kingston avenues Lance and big bro Jermaine/

Yeah, I have been in the hurricane/

My closest wanted to leave me believe me cause they failed to see the vision/

All they saw was the nightmare, my failures and mis steps/

My walk has not been perfect, I question daily being a father/

Want to know what goes through a man's head who says why bother/

I was the residue of bad parenting so I'm willing cross any bridge to be better/

I don't write this for likes or hearts/

I write just to write and share something real in a fake world/

Everybody fronting like they are Pablo Escobar/

And it's a war on the colors going on so what you are eating isn't going make me go/

So why feed me your timeline when God is looking/

And the devil is cooking our souls on a pedestal/

So, I will be one of few praying for peace/

Praying that you understand there is something evil in the air/

Where love isn't wanted/

Gucci is flaunted/

And I smell the bullshit on the net/

Selfishness leading many to the abyss when the last kiss goodnight wanders over muddy waters/

It's a black mama twerking with her back out for some dollars/

Daddy is in jail trying to provide for a family tainted by sin/

And revelations is a chapter looking realer each day that passes/

There are no classes for saving you/

Your uncle is getting high on the money made selling something stolen out of your house/

Mom is crying in her blouse cause the house was aflame/

And God woke you up in the middle of the night choking on smoke/

Yeah, I was broke family and only The Father could fix me/

Yeah, I lived a life where the heart could have lay broken/

But I joined the MTA and made my own token/

I'm praying you understand I was dipped in anger from a time where I caught my mommas side piece hiding naked in my bedroom/

Tears running down my face/

And it doesn't hurt anymore to take you to that place/

All apart of spilling the blood of my poetry/

Watching your twin boys birthed at a time where they only weighed a pound/

And they lay them naked on your chest so they can hear the sound your heart makes/

In that place you can feel the power of God/

And you may not believe, because you haven't seen enough to deter you/

But I put myself on the cross my fam to CURE YOU!

AGAIN

I asked my MAGA hat wearing brother/

Why wear that?

And he said because of the hue like you/

I sat back and examined his mix like DJ clue/

And it's true the reason he is paying child support is because his black woman cheated on him with his black brother/

Don't forget it was his black mother that abused him/

It was a black stranger slipping on black ice in front of his home that sued him/

It was a black gun from a black kid that shot his cousin/

Black classmate playing teasing about his hand me downs/

It was a black cop with a bogus parking ticket that got him/

It was a black handled knife at his throat when a group of black teens robbed him/

It was a Black Friday years ago/

Back when he sported a black Afro/

So, I have to excuse him when he wears his white shoes and under his feet are his black blues/

And he is going to make sure every black man gets to know what happened to him/

He is just doing his part with every fiber of his black pain/

Dancing in the rain having the world think that he is insane/

But God sees you/

The ignorant believe you/

Silly man you let the devil deceive you/

Only the good lord can alleviate you/

None of the black women you love could take you/

Now we are all stuck with this fake you/

This person everyone loathes and doesn't know what to

make of you/

And I have to defend you and all I can do is hope to God

that he makes you great - AGAIN!

PART IV -

Fire

Fire

Forged in the pits of share cropping/

I know my father wished for better days/

Behind the plow of a mule/

I know he prayed for brighter days/

And better ways to earn a living/

Under the clear blue skies/

A man tries to be free bootlegging Gin to begin with/

Earned enough to gift a trip to Harlem/

Under those same skies I know my mother wanted to be free/

Running away from a strict Jehovah household/

Where Christmas was a sin and birthdays are never celebrated/

She grew to resent the unfairness/

Ran away to Mount Vernon where she grew to be

something other than a witness/

But those southern winds guide me on days where

Brooklyn lets those bullets fly/

I look to the sky and I can feel the spirit of resilience/

The smell of cotton and tobacco swirls through the winds/

The devil himself lends his ear/

Promises of money and glory/

But lies live and burn in the – FIRE!

WORTHLESS

I wrote my story in a tabernacle I hemmed/

There were sharks and horrible things in the waters I had to swim/

I know that the picture is bigger than projected/

We passed down our pain and misfortune/

Our parents failed but forgive them for they knew not what they did/

Mistakes so minuscule so they were easy to be hid/

But we reaped what they sowed/

We laid in the grass they mowed/

Then we planted our own seeds in the mess hoping it grow/

So, we buy more Jordan's and B.S. we never had/

Take more trips abroad but forget to carry the Lord/

In a world where nothing is sacred anymore/

Love don't live here no more/

The residue of death lay on the floor/

The blood of a princely moor runs through my core/

I see clearly when the Lord is near me/

A lot of you pretending to be Christian/

But your heart and soul is missing/

Sitting on the dock of the bay angry at the world/

When the you in you don't belong in you/

And your swimming in earthly possessions/

Yet you haven't learned from your lessons/

Life is a fleeting moment on a sinking ship/

Love, laugh and share/

Take care of the ones taking care of you/

It's a sad way to go without someone who loves you holding you/

I'm older now with more substance in the stuff I spew/

Nothing new I'm just reminding most of you that the road isn't paved neatly for us/

There are bumps and dips/

Falls and slips/

A paycheck with no tips/

I'm holding on to something greater/

Cause I saw the bottom of my barrel/

I saw the bullet looking back at me/

And I saw the tears from three kids who had to endure like me/

From losing a parent at a young age due to depression/

Due to opioid abuse and alcohol misuse/

That's before the crisis and Isis/

The lie is it will get better but not without someone to lean on/

Just make sure your holding on to something Holy and not something solely soulless/

Beauty is only skin deep, it's what lay beneath the surface that determines what the worth is/

Truth is that in this social media world, most of are too fake and WORTHLESS!

RAISE THEM

Blood on the pavement/

Seems the Lord came to save men/

But my people still in chains slaving/

For the descendants of cave men/

Bullets in the air/

The echo of gunfire in the rear/

Little man felt the fire before the gun flare/

In the ambulance he laid stretched out in his underwear/

My words write his eulogy/

Whispers of the dead taken too soon is nothing new to me/

Another king killed in the community he tried to uplift/

He tried to help his hood with his gift/

And you wonder why our talent is moving out faster than a

Lyft/

I sift through the sands of time/

Praying for the heartless in my kingdom hearts/

Mama can you see the blood spilled over the seven deadly

sins?/

It's all relative when your distant cousin wants your life/

But never did the time/

Never saw you covered in muck and slime/

Never saw your tears in the darkness/

Never saw you limp, crawl to your stall/

Never saw you on your knees praying for change like Sam

Cooke/

Never took a look at your struggle that forged the diamond

you are/

There's people wishing for clean water to drink/

You're wasting your prayers on a new sink/

A new mink over the whip lashes/

Hope dashed over a small African boy in a diamond mine/

While demons like Rockefeller gets their name uttered after

death/

Watching the rat race in the morning like a visionary

overlooking the matrix/

Dr. Sebi said the only disease is mucus/

But I like beef cake Brutus/

Man what kind of game is this they don't even have to

shoot us/

Their whole ideology pollutes us/

So I'm still going to fight to awaken you true Hebrews

from your slumber/

John 3:16 is your daily number/

Don't die from hunger in the game/

The mockingbird sings a sad song in a cage/

A thot has a expiration date don't limit yourself princess to

your looks/

Real men like women who love a Good book/

Praise him/

Rest In Peace To all our fallen/

May their stars never dim, Amen/

Put your hands up America/

Wakanda forever - RAISE THEM!

OVERCOMING

Some thought I got too sentimental/

But I dumped the rental on the FDR/

Swerved in the lane/

They said I didn't sell well/

But my soul never fell for a dollar/

Those push-ups at night are meant to invite spirits of

warriors before/

Yet still rock a fedora while watching Dora the explorer

with my daughter/

The order is broken/

The youths are smoking and drinking/

Thinking they are only going live once/

But I'm putting my ticket in with God to last forever/

In the cosmos lighting the way for the Bonner's that follow/

My soul was hollow, so racked in pain/

Away from southern comfort I had to rely on my anger/

The danger was, I lost my way alone in the darkness where

many men end/

Hand gripping a cold glass of hen/

I chose to fight to begin again/

No roadmap to win again/

Seen close friends disappear in thin air like a finger snap

from Thanos/

I wish you could have seen us in our glory in 390/

Hat tilted, cross colour and boss wear/

Razor tucked, no religion/

Walkman in hand while we walked man/

Dreams of us all rising and in our youthful grandeur/

Hands slapping the back of ones neck, and wearing out the

substitute teacher/

There was joy in our laughter/

Rest In Peace to Barbara, gone never forgotten/

The roses are never rotten/

We're still here riding the seven seas/

Fishing with chuck and Kenny/

Exploding on the scene like TNT/

I hope the world knows we were meant to be more than just

a footnote on Brooklyn's eulogy/

We were soldiers in a war zone and walked with the dead/

Before the night king raised them/

We praised them and honored them by OVERCOMING!

MALL

"White lips, pale face breathing in the snowflakes"/

Love lost, time takes/

Broken heart, plates breaks/

Moon shines over drunk lakes/

The stakes are high/

The good die/

The evil suffer with all that life makes/

The river dried/

The liquor rose/

They tagged the toes/

No dream there grows/

Just weeds in the ground/

Nothing was the sound/

In loneliness they passed no one around/

No one holding their hand as they crossed into the light/

Not right/

But not wrong/

Sad song/

Tears fall, casket made six long/

Prayers washed ashore/

Here today, tomorrow no more/

In the sky we hoped for/

A sign to guide us to hopes door/

Worlds cruel/

Spiritual duel/

Screams for help in a dark alley/

Prayers lost, faith shaken/

Souls snatched, taken/

So many burning over the lake and/

I can't save you all/

Cause you have to want something eternal that you can't

ever buy in a MALL!

BEST

They ask me why I'm tired/

But I have been in the game longer than stringer bell was
wired/

My hopes and dreams were fired then rehired/

My supplier of hope died on a cross/

I may have forfeited, but I never loss/

Of course you are going to hear a lie/

But my heart lives in the truth and I will die in the booth/

Book and pencil in hand writing scriptures you can't
understand/

I walk on air, sea and land/

I forgot the notes because I was kicked out the band at a
stage where teens begin to age/

But I started playing the blues with clues written in the
stars/

My heart cries for healing/

I'm losing all my feeling/

Loves arrows leave me reeling/

The paint of perfection on my walls are peeling/

I pay homage to a football player still kneeling/

How can we stop all the killing in chi town?/

A little baby shot and you don't notice it because it's not

your town/

A future snuffed out before his dream formed/

But I get the delusional label because I'm praying to God

for peace/

Fully knowing he's able/

Or is my faith a fable/

Did Martin die for us to have cable?/

Did Malcolm die for us to have fake love and hip hop?/

Do you ignore my screams in the abyss?/

Because it doesn't put gifts in your house for Christmas?/

I'm tied to the cosmos/

A rose is still a rose even if its weary/

My eyes are teary/

I know it's hard to bare me/

But I have seen the future and it scares me/

Even when the Lord prepares me/

In the presence of my enemies in the middle of hades/

He anoints my head with oil/

My dead thrives in the soil/

My anger makes my blood boil/

Walking toward the nooses with bruises on my heart/

Cleared ready to depart with the spirit of Carmichael and

Bonner family crests tatted in my chest/

Still trying to pass the test

Still I have my bow and arrow aimed on one thing being

the - BEST!

NIGHTMARE

Can you see the blood on that American flag/

The blood of black, white, yellow and blue/

Under the idea of freedom/

Under the guise of liberty/

Under the stars at night/

Dog tags hung on a rifle helmet in tow/

Even when the leader is a buffoon/

We march, we step in beat/

Under the desert heat and frozen tundra/

Under Gods thunder and the Lords rain/

How do we honor our brave men and women/

Our brothers in arms/

Who give the ultimate sacrifice for a lie to be free/

To come home to a country where it's forbidden to take a
knee/

Excuse me but the smell is tainted with bull dung/

And cold Big Macs with chicken nuggets/

In a country built on being free it seems to me they're

building walls to keep us in/

In poverty, in slumlord habitats/

Sleeping in the street along with the alley cats/

Still saluting a flag that stands for liberty and justice for all/

For all if you can afford to believe it/

Look around America you have failed your mission/

And we all are praying, wishing you honor yourself/

You honor the fallen soldier who died for a dream/

A dream that we all can't see because we are living a -

NIGHTMARE!

PART V-

Slipping

SLIPPING

These are the tears of my brother/

The want for the pain to cease/

And dreams to turn true/

To spread our wings and fly when our gray skies turn to

blue/

To escape a reality where we feel oppressed/

A place where our future does not feel possessed/

Where every day we feel like Walter from Raisin in The

Sun/

We all want our mothers to believe in us/

Even when we are strong and wrong/

We all want to sing and dance to our own song/

When the pressures of the world push us down/

It's always nice to have someone hold you down/

We all need to feel like a king with a new crown/

Especially when –

It feels like a world war/

And you don't even know what you're fighting for/

Lost in a cycle of despair/

Turn on the news only to feel worse/

Little kid dead from a automatic gun burst/

Too young to be in a hearse/

Young girl lost in a world/

Where men rape you with stares/

Put a pill in your drink and steal your virginity, yet it feels like no one cares/

Where you don't feel safe to walk at night unless you're in pairs/

Every woman walks with fears/

Walks with years of degradation/

Mix that with alienation, sexism and racism/

Now you have a weapon of mass destruction armed to explode/

A gun in her purse ready to reload/

A world on the brink about to implode/

While each of us race through the matrix trying to avoid -

SLIPPING!

BEGINS

Woke up 4:44/

I had to give you more/

More me, no story/

I do this for more than me/

For you/

My baby Aria, same hue as blue/

Running off the plug with no DJ, no clue/

These verses are sick, ah-choo/

I grew from the same dirt and hurt as king Jay/

Those that knew me would say/

That my run was poetic and prophetic/

And I did this with no credit/

I'm writing in my tablet like a coke feen with a habit/

Reaching for the stars, I got to have it/

Somebody get Spike Lee/

I thought me making it wasn't likely/

Boys and Girls High/

Kangaroo pride and joy of bed sty/

On a red eye to the Carolinas/

I side swiped a few vaginas/

But my heart beats for the twins, Aria and you/

My heart was thrown in the ocean its true/

Somewhere in Macys downtown my world was turned

upside down/

I been had this poetry crown/

Birthed from gin, I didn't know where to begin/

On a stage in Harlem headband over my brow/

Spitting my venom steady/

Even back then I wasn't ready/

Each syllable was riddled by an individual who lacked the

residual knowledge now possessed/

Each word I molest/

In the finest denim I possess/

In the flesh, these hazel eyes hold a surprise only the

hoodlums can arise/

My anger, my pain a constant thing/

Blood on my wedding ring - period/

Tears over my casket but it was all a dream/

We walk with our demise not truly ready/

Knowing that these streets are deadly/

Finished my degree on Marcy Avenue/

After quitting over the body of my best friend/

It took old boys high to rescue me/

I was supposed to fail, end up in jail like Browder/

But I was born special like powder/

I walk with the ghosts of every kid from 390/

Jansport strings floating in the air/

Albany houses in my rear/

But I belong to Bergen Street/

Please mama don't fall, take my seat/

The odds I did beat/

Like an inmate does his meat/

At the gates of hell ready to greet/

With this cross in my hand and all these angelic minions I

command/

I got 44 days to show my enemies 44 ways to meet their

last days/

4:44 in the evening/

Seeing is believing/

Don't plan on leaving my twins and Aria grieving/

You can get a glimpse of me fleeing in a Benz/

I'm going to see the twins grow from boys to men's/

Every story ends, but at 4:44 in the morning mines -

BEGINS

FLY

I was naive I believe/

Thought love could be caught, captured and bought/

But Love is free and runs to the warmest embrace/

Under moonlight hands caressing face/

In between satin sheets and shivering ecstasy/

Over dreams dashed against the dunes/

While soft tunes utter "I'll make love to you"/

Where the strongest men bend the knee/

And it forces you to be more than you were destined to be/

Where family ties the knot/

Then you work so hard you forgot how you started/

Where the Red Sea parted/

And you suffocated each other's pain until it departed/

Then we become pain restarted because you forget that
love sacrifices/

Its free and in bondage at the same time/

Twisted together in the same line/

Flying through the air like Jon Snow and Daenerys/

And as scary as the ride is, you stay on because true love

endures/

It survives the storms and the struggles/

Only with God can it grow stronger/

Only with prayer can it outlast the neonatal intensive C - U/

Only with hope can you see through the fog/

Where you run to each other's arms not jog/

Where with sword in hand you fight the rising tide/

Along with ego and pride and close friends who like to

divide/

In the solitude of a starry night you have to decide/

Whether in the end you're going to ride or die/

Whether we use our wings like dragons and we sink into

the frigid ocean/

Or rise up over Westeros and - FLY!

HEAR IT

Up late with the devil/

He is talking about wilding out/

I'm reading the scriptures trying to chill out/

Them ghosts they never sleep, they are still out/

Talking bout you can't continue this path/

I sit back and laugh/

Two hundred push-ups later killing my wrath/

In the house alone examining each pimple in my dimple/

Life used to be simple when the sound of music banged out

my speaker/

Before failure and strife became my substitute teacher/

In Gods arms I laid arms splayed/

My mother abused pills before this crisis/

Bombs over my childhood before Isis/

My words scribbled on the pad bred to be the nicest/

Twice this clock struck my aorta/

This court is out of order/

On the border I lay building my own wall of solitude/

Bergen Street raised me/

Old exes played me/

Those bullets missed me lady/

Broken glass on the floor/

One hour before four and death knocks on my door/

No mas no more por favor/

This will go down in urban lore/

Like a unsmoked loosie out the store/

My core is filled with the spirit/

When I open my mouth I hope and pray you see not only

the truth but you HEAR IT!

PAIN

I am not going to sit here and act like I want to be messiah/

I got the urge to be a pariah/

My fire is ignited by pain and deceit/

Hard to measure that kind of heat/

Flames secrete from each heartbeat/

No trick or treat to this feat/

I close my eyes and see the dead smile/

I'm walking my own green mile in a style you wouldn't

want to copy/

Each drop of me has been touched by the devil but blessed

by God/

Odd, but my hymns are sung in the fires of hades/

In the back of a stolen Mercedes/

My passion is insatiable/

Racing a bull that looks like me down a lonely highway/

Don't even know if I made it this far my way/

Praying for the path to become bearable/

Put my life line in a parable/

And life itself is a short task/

I bask in Gods glory/

Hard to think I'm not even the author of my own story/

Each scribble was influenced by a higher power/

The whole school laughed at me when Principal Joe Clark

said I only passed lunch/

Hard to Lean on Me after that/

Watched my angels become demons/

Found myself baptized in holy water/

But the flames never wither/

God is a giver/

Cause now I shape the flames into words that burn the

pages/

The mic is left smoking on stages/

The cage is a lonely place/

Picked up a college degree at a pace not ideal/

But it hangs on my wall so it's real/

But even after the math is done/

It's just me walking on the sun/

Unscathed by the fire/

A true Phoenix in his genius/

Rising from the ashes of misfortune and - PAIN!

FIND US

Walking on the edge of the birth of an inferno/

Mesmerized by watching it burn slow/

Don't know where to go while the cauldron smokes and the

brimstone blazes/

Inside of me lay a fire of emotion/

The notion that I was weakened by life is a sight fabricated

under the moonlight/

It's not too soon to tell you that this man is hiding a

werewolf/

On top of my building screaming for freedom/

Looking at the stars wanting to be them/

Yearning to hang in the night sky illuminating the path for

my seeds/

Maybe just maybe they could grow to where the chains

don't exist/

Not shot by dirty cops saying they were resist - ing/

I'm daydreaming of a day where my other half holds me/

Dreaming of a place where heaven folds me delicately/

Brooklyn is the birthplace of my Truth/

The transit system here nurtured me in a booth/

And my only token is that I haven't started smoking/

The pain of yesterday I left in Gods arms just today/

Hoping that all the emotions left in me could bring out the

best in me/

All the success is God blessing me/

All the struggles is him testing me/

I'm living each day trying to be the best in me/

I watched my mother succumb to prescription pills before

the opioids were a crisis/

I prayed on knees for all the kids hurting like me to help

angels align us/

But the gangs, money and ghetto BS tried to blind us/

Still we had guardian angels trying to mind us/

Each of us carrying a security blanket from the past like

Linus/

On the graduation podium with a smile painted that binds

us/

In adulthood I find myself on older knees praying for them

same angels to - FIND US!

TALL

Wet silhouettes fall upon the gravel/

The webs spun together begins to unravel/

The sun becomes forgotten when hopes and dreams rotten/

The bliss of a welcome kiss becomes this haven of torture/

The ensnaring of false caring/

Where lies take root and choke out the truth/

And the body dies with no heart/

No sequel to this part, finito/

Nothing here to repeat though/

The shades of a soldiers are bloody and haunted/

The task I was placed with was daunted/

The jewels we obtained were flaunted/

Rivers run into an empty ocean/

It's easy, very easy to lose focus/

We cry at night praying for Jesus to hold us/

And in the morn wake us like Foldgers/

They labeled me great and my debate is I'm just like you/

I have stumbled, fell and scraped my knee/

Hell I get lost in this wilderness just being me/

My degree is a useless associate to my presence/

My present to you has always been my truth unloaded in a

booth/

What is love, "baby don't hurt me no more"/

Just a night at the Roxbury/

Trying to bury my past in a dirty trash bag/

Burning the ashes of the dead that live on in my head/

Alone is where you'll find me pondering on my solitude/

A solid dude but my heart is weary/

My anger has subdued but there are a few who should fear

me/

I want to be care free but that is not me/

I get angry at the news of a child abused/

I get sad at the thought of a kid crying over his mother's

casket/

Yet some will label me a basket case/

A case debated on Capitol Hill/

Undeterred with vision blurred/

I doubt if I can win again/

My hazel eyes reddened with D'ussie and cola/

Don't worry about me I was forged in a place where the

heat melted dreams/

Shoot I was not even supposed to get this far/

Visions of a sixteen year old me burning in a stolen crashed

Honda/

Bullets in my chest trying to suppress a father's death/

My last breath has been delayed by my will to not die on

Bergen street/

I'm here over the spirit of what was/

Explosions in the rear/

A black hoodie over my stare/

The devil pointing his finger at me/

But I was bathed in holy water/

So he can't the climb the walls that border me even if he

can touch those closest to me/

I light a candle and say the lord is my Shepherd and he laid

me down in green pastures/

And if even if the Bonner's fall/

They will rise out of the ashes with me standing - TALL!

PART VI -

The City

The City

40 years deep/

They 40 years sleep/

The love for this misplaced/

I pissed on the wall of poetry until its defaced/

Placed my hymns on the brims of hip hop/

And you flip flop on the hate/

Been this long, I can wait for my name to be mentioned
among the great/

One thing is for sure/

I mixed theses lines with pure heart and soul/

Stirred in a bowl and served it hot and cold/

My rib cage explodes and my heart expires over the wires/

The heavens open the doors to welcome home my soul/

The respect is over-due/

The false judgements about me are frivolous/

I only highlighted the real in us/

The ups and downs/

Pitfalls and crowns/

The ghetto and the countries light and dark hues/

Over melancholy blues/

Danced in MJ shoes while the glitter faded/

Yeah, I am jaded/

My hopes and dreams spaded/

My just desserts evaded/

Still elated cause I made it somehow/

In spite of it all/

I took my ball like LeBron and dunked it on the lies told/

My stature is bold regardless of how cold the weather is/

The betrayal by my closest swift/

I revenged the stabs in the back with my gift/

Even if it's never read nightly/

I put my footprint in the sand and a boot in the devil's ass

at Sunday mass/

And I did it with such class and grace/

That my shoe polish is the taste/

So, you can sit on your stool/

And talk against me/

But there is no love lost/

I paid the cost/

Cause my soul was lost in the heart of - THE CITY!

BLUE

Picture us together under the red moon/

On our knees praying for a better future/

All while the world around us slowly burns down/

And I look up like Pendergrass and "the whole town is

laughing at me"/

Our hearts melting in a symphony of tears, laughter, joy

and pain/

The Lords rain falling upon us steadily/

The world depended on me heavily/

I admit that my walk in the past wasn't heavenly/

But my medley of life has been my truth even when I

walked this road lonely/

Before my savior got the chance to know me/

After the dead reached out their hands to hold me/

I laid to rest the weak old me/

And I raise my head to the heavens while the waves around

me crash in/

I hope you all know that the best things in life don't involve

cash and it's beautiful/

It's humbling and noteworthy/

Too many of you non believing even when Gods touch

carries you while you're grieving/

When the pain is unbearable/

He made you still able/

That there is proof - no fable/

No alcohol soothes me truly/

I have made this walk of faith my duty/

So while the facade of the ghost of Eric dissipates in my

own infinity war/

Still a black panther at my core/

Fighting to captain America and more/

I know being a Aries makes me more Hulk than Thor/

But I rep New York City like the Fantastic Four/

Ever since my music teacher Mr. Nor made me a guardian

of the galaxy in G Flat/

My Hawkeye made the notes flow in my soul/

Never knew that the sound of music would be stolen/

Never knew that my heart could be so controlling/

I wanted Jr and my brother to fit my mold and/

The circle of trust shattered from meeting my parents out of

the womb glass of gin in hand/

Strapped to my cross at a loss of words/

My dreams flutter through the night sky/

From Brooklyn to Dubai/

I'm just a reflection of us melting under prayers for each

other/

Intertwined under the cover/

Where lover gets twisted with friend/

Where we lay naked under marital bliss and a wet kiss/

Hoping to discover a better me and a better you/

Where our gray skies turn and stay - BLUE!

13

I have been thinking about you for thirteen days/

Trying to be your sunshine in thirteen ways/

Trying to be your Shakespeare so I wrote thirteen plays/

And i have been a pain in your ass served on thirteen trays/

But I have honored you daily even if I caused you pain/

I tried to be your tree even when the winds nearly broke me/

No need to quote me/

I have been torn in two but I'm trying to make you happy but that's hard when the winds are snappy/

But I wouldn't change much in these thirteen years except the car/

That was the spark that wedged us far/

But know this, I'm always trying to be your star when the lights dim/

Trying to be your life jacket when the waters get too deep too swim/

And I don't sing love songs/

But I know how to make sweet music/

I know how to kiss your spirit and ignite flames/

I'm just hoping you'll be my golden girl in thirteen more years/

If god lets my clouds disappear/

I hope you'll be here to hear the cheers/

When I climb this mountain of life and plant my flag/

And you can have 13 red roses/

Make love in 13 poses/

Close the ship and sail like 13 Moses/

Forget my 13 deficiencies/

And look upon my 13 good tendencies/

Sit on the beach holding hands over 13 memories/

We all know I'm battling me/

Truth is I'm close to victory/

And my history is written/

My scars are not hidden/

I have laid out my soul bare/

I hope and pray I gave you 13 reasons like MJ to be there/

When the next thirteen years gets - HERE!

My Halo

Forgive my hiatus/

Spent time dissecting the greatest/

Life treating my team like cheese trying to grate us/

Goons outside trying to waste us/

Police kicking in my door trying to mace us/

The government outside my hood trying to displace us/

My enemies lined up trying to race us/

Mask on scared to face us/

Cause I am fighting for my people I am labeled a racist/

But believe me in my heart when it comes to poetry I am the
greatest/

Jay said this was all a dream/

Covered in blood can you hear me scream/

I hope the lord see a brother trying to redeem/

Things ain't always what it seems/

Graffiti paints my tomb/

Alone in death, you can find me strapped to my gloom/

Fighting ghosts from my past/

Forty years in this field I don't know how much longer I can last/

Back then I wore knock off gear in front of the class/

Hoping to wake from my slumber/

Put a dollar on a number/

Exchange my hunger for hope/

Outlined my vision with dope/

Gun on the table trying to cope/

Visions of my awakening in the middle of this wasteland/

Touched by a hand that understands/

Tears fall on my face from a place where I learned heartache and pain/

This scripture is just a piece of my peace/

Trapped in this beast tied to a cross/

At a loss for words at times/

I lace each of these poetic rhymes with a fragment of my entity/

Just to let the world know the devil and God lives in me/

Still trying to find out in this dream what I am meant to be/

Love, pain, anger, regret, remorse, happiness, joy, sadness and
depression was all that the lord sent to me/

Believe me world/

In the real world I am a king, ascribe and a friend/

But in this fantasy I am hurt and broken to no end/

My heart is in ICU trying to mend/

Fighting constantly at every bend/

Praying on knees knowing I am not worthy for God to send me –
MY HALO!

FIGHT

She said "she wasn't much for poetry"/

She didn't like to read/

Instead she cut herself at night and watch her blood bleed/

She lived vicarious through friends so a man she didn't
need/

She danced with her emotions at night and daydreamed on
one word succeed/

She wasn't one for politics, barely watched the news/

Knew her place and held no ground/

Men raped her past and she made no sound/

Muffled her screams and made it seem li a bad dream/

Tears would fall suddenly when the barriers cracked/

The world was stacked against her/

Her own betrothed was baffled/

She raffled off time/

Dabbled in crime/

Sold her own innocence for a dime when times were hard/

She twisted and turned to no end/

Did a line of coke cause her heart could not mend/

She couldn't pretend anymore/

Love she didn't recognize it at her door/

Siphoned money off her family/

To her own kids she became a stranger/

She was just another girl on the IRT alone by herself in the winters night/

She knew nothing of God/

But with her last breath she still saw the light/

Cause God still covers sinners when they have no strength to - FIGHT

AMEN

They prayed and put hands on the lost maiden/

She thought she was strong/

She would never cave in/

But loneliness caught her in a place where she could save men/

They ended the prayer in Amen/

The reason alone is why men slay men/

Believed a lie from an ex spurned, for her turn she was just waiting/

He was trying to end the pain in his heart, made a message with regret he was just stating/

Alone in her anger at a Days Inn/

Her matrimony now longer holy its grip fading/

The lightening of the stranger's smile entranced her like a bolt from Raiden/

She never was the type to play men/

But she wanted to feel a spark in the darkness her heart played in/

She danced on in heat in his strong arms she laid in/

Love lost in intercourse the course got a star grading/

Different from the usual intimate saving/

The ground was new with fresher paving/

Questions of her whereabouts now needed evading/

And the soul gets lost in the game she was playing/

Lost notes found under the armoire on the ground they were just laying/

A heart broke he worked his butt off is all he kept saying/

I watch his eyes dance red and his heart breaking/

I knew that place well and I knew that it was dangerous to

stay in/

I grabbed his hands and prayed for his soul to have peace

and keep him the same way God made him/

His anger faded with her pregnant embrace the gun fell

from his hands and we ended our prayer in - AMEN!

I CAN'T BREATHE

I clap my hands and watch the dust settle/

Pedal to the metal/

The fire in me still burns steady/

I'm going as far as God lets me/

My walk has been deadly mixed with a medley of beautiful

moments/

Tokens to let me know he is still here/

Where a mother no longer breathes air/

She beats the drum of a heart where the vessels thin out/

I been in a bout, a duel/

Played the fool/

Failed playing it cool/

Contemplated life greatest mysteries on the stool/

Wondered how much greater I'm going to have to be for you all to notice me/

For you to notice the fortitude hidden in me/

How the Lord projects himself in me/

Lights flashing in the nights sky/

Restoration plaza middle of bed sty/

A little version of me making a payment agreement with con Ed/

Now the dead light my path/

And I have bundled my wrath like Naruto/

My lyrics shoot though from here to Pluto/

Still I -

Look to the sky for answers/

Just to walk away with more questions/

More lessons unlearned/

The cross burned in my yard with the sign MAGA rules/

Simple fools in simple bigotry/

Stupidity is the tapestry/

America the great calamity/

Too much hate, no need to debate/

And at this rate we will never awaken from this state of anarchy/

Forgive me officer I thought that a banned hold means illegal/

Don't mind me, I'm just the humble voice of the people/

Suffocating here and still - I CAN'T BREATHE!

PART VII -

Heard Them

Say

Heard Them Say

My lyrics flood the Sahara and the cotton fields of Edenton/

Some of you caught in between the line that the Democrats
and Republicans created/

Mixing God with liquor/

Evil men pretend to be God like/

Good men hide behind their charity/

I was a casualty before the age of twelve/

Every little step taken in the valley of death/

The burden of carrying hopes and dreams alive for folks
not here/

It's a strain, can't complain my verses rain forty days and
nights/

The lights of a pandemic city shine against my aura/

I'm destined for greatness Miss America/

The letters spell fate/

The hate was a debate cause black folks all want to be

great/

But few follow their dreams off the top of the building/

I'm dying with each feeling/

The paint on the ceiling is still peeling/

I was in to dealing weed, wasn't good so now I'm pedaling

perseverance when the sign reads no clearance/

The interference came in a red dress I guess/

The road shakes and quivers/

A soft kiss on a pillow can create tremors and palpitations/

 The stations get skipped/

While Emmitt Till whistles a lullaby/

The white sheets are replaced with a badge and a gun/

Now Jim Crow doesn't have to run/

The colors get mixed and the messages lost in an African Holocaust/

The cost is souls and pain/

The hungry walk the streets robbing, stealing and killing/

The homework gets completed by street light/

The dream is deferred/

The vision of what we were blurred along with the lines of success/

The river runs deep brother is what – I HEARD THEM SAY!

SENTENCE

I watch as my coffin drifts in the air/

Wonder if the dead see, speak and hear/

Evil sits in a corner with an ice-cold stare/

The outerwear is out of here/

Wonder if the dead dress to impress/

Or do they walk in the flesh chains rattling through our

Christmas Carol/

Can Tiny Tim ignore deaths silence through the Radio

waves like Imus/

I'm just pontificating my demise through curious eyes/

No Benjamin Button surprise/

Thou have seen me forlorn and ecstatic/

With my take and turns dramatic/

And the static in my residence is antagonistic to my smile/

I still find a way to parlay peace in unfriendly waters/

Nothing is perfect except pain/

It's runs through us all like a virus unleashed/

The world released its venom of racism and we wore it like denim/

The rhythm of hip hop blared through the speaker/

Fist raised to the blue sky still trying figure why we are still fighting the power at the eleventh hour/

Martin Luther's dream died in Memphis/

We just fired the apprentice/

Then watch the badge wearers Lynch us/

America need not wait for reparations they just bench us/

And world war three will start at the completion of this – SENTENCE!

JOY

Osirus and Anubis hid away in tombs/

The sarcophagus was decorated/

The life lived celebrated/

We were fated to meet here at the door guarding the

heavens stargate/

Roses litter the pavement/

The music was heavenly and stale/

The rider on the horse was pale/

The other three were too far off to tell/

He met me while I engaged in prayer/

Sword in hand dripped crimson/

I looked in his eyes/

And I saw all my dreams fade/

Everything I hoped and cared for withered in his gaze/

The days became a moment of finality/

Looked up to the night stars and made my final wish/

That the path that chose me was never full of carnage and pain/

Lost my grandparents as they witnessed Jehovah/

I lost my mother after she lost her mind/

I lost a brother to country and flag and another to a gang of another flag/

Dag, supposedly mistaken identity/

I always felt I was meant to be more/

But my hands were tied to heaven's door/

But as the sword swings/

An angel sings/

I guess when you walk with the Lord even death brings -

JOY!

GREATNESS

I saw the rose pedals fall like red raindrops/

Over the casket/

Only thirteen, but I would lose every teen year after/

Suppressed my sadness and anger with laughter/

That chapter of life I didn't speak on it enough in my own

book/

Thrown out of music class and sent to E2/

Chasing a vision of love too young for Reno/

But God will remove people who don't belong on your trip/

And I joined a gang of fools like a Crip/

Stole bikes armed with a baseball bat/

My karma came swiftly, jumped while the police turned the

other way/

Walked away with no bruise except an ego already
shattered/

A life lived battered/

Poetry found me with a knife up my sleeve/

The verses poured from wounds that time couldn't heal/

I learned how to carry my cross and deal/

Make each scar apart of my shield/

And the mighty Excalibur I was finally able to wield/

I'm still playing in my field of dreams/

All while the ghetto screams/

An angelic mother's smile beams/

So many threw me in the trash heap/

In the muck and slime/

Covered in shit, I gave my pain rhythm and rhyme/

In a place and time where likes overpowered love/

I illuminated a dark place and raised up a dark race/

When I retire in life, I hope you trace the tracks of my tears/

And it leads you to - GREATNESS!

STAY

When is it more than just words on a paper?/

When the story makes a tear drop from your eye/

Or a smile born out of your storm?/

What makes these verses more than letters combined?/

Is it the kiss forgotten when marriage hits rock bottom?/

Is it a touch gone cold in a world gone crazy?/

Is it the joy in a babies eyes described in detail?/

Is it possessions bought like retail?/

Is it that we are all damaged and used?/

With more pain inside and egos bruised/

We went from classy to trashy like love and hip hop/

Still missing my own Jimmy while with age my set dip/

There's a war outside and we are steady killing inside the club/

Loves one stolen, all while the police patrolling/

They are controlling the narrative like Dolan/

So, you only hear what big brother wants you to hear/

We forgot to hold the things that are really precious dear/

Too busy holding on to things that are material/

Can't mess up those Jordan's or Air Force ones/

While the crooked cops and fake gangsters out here shooting our sons, because we didn't teach them smarter/

Too many innocent martyrs/

Not enough change to make a dollar/

Too much poverty in a world where our worth is worn/

My poor heart is torn on a rainy morn/

Am I wrong for being angry and faithful in a world where evil prevailed?/

And the good are not just dying young/

They are killing themselves and I understand/

So many stories and to me the words are always more than words on the paper/

They always touch my spirit/

And the pain and sadness reverberate in my soul/

I lose control of who and what God made me/

I close my eyes and realize the only thing I own is the air he gave me/

I fall to my knees hoping he can save me/

The blood of more than just my poetry spills in the darkness/

I just hope that it sparks the imagination of a brighter day/

The world has lost its way and the sun has gone away/

I just hope these gray skies are not here to - STAY!

WORDS

The waves shatter against the concrete/

The world trembles and shakes in its wake/

The break in my subconscious came as the bodies piled/

The number dialed for prayers and emergencies

outnumbered angel wings/

The tide that rode in brings death among other things/

The rich mixed the poor in the reservoir/

The store left looted/

The land polluted/

The revelry and beauty of life taken away in a blast that its

radius couldn't be measured/

Without the tragedy the things that really matter couldn't

be treasured/

God is watching us all/

The call most if not all of us missed/

Too busy on material things wished/

Too busy trying get likes amongst the strikes/

On knees I prayed for peace amongst war/

The things precious are not found in a store/

The precious material things litter the floor when we don't

them anymore/

Our collective heart rotten to the core/

Sell out for less than a dollar/

I ask the father for vision and clarity/

The pain is married to me/

The past carries me/

The present battles me/

The future a fallacy/

I tread where the rattle be/

Holding on to a broken cross at a loss for - WORDS!

BE

Listen closely/

It's old Brooklyn you see when I walk/

It's North Carolina you hear when I talk/

It's gunfire my enemies see when I write, then the chalk/

Bred in the pit/

Indian style when I sit/

And I admit I get questioned if this is all legit/

My grit and grime was forged in rhyme/

But it didn't happen overnight it took time/

It took pain, rum and wine/

Yeah girl, these hazel eyes are mine/

Alfredo with chicken when I dine/

Spent my summers in a place where you can smell the pine/

Away from the crack war behind my door/

Albany, St. Marks and more/

Young black men dead over white powder/

Just a reminder of white power/

Cocaine, sugar and flour/

That's crack, diabetes and they still get the cake/

We are designed to make an excuse for systematic abuse/

What's the use, most say of just trying/

Our numbers are depleting, we're dying/

Everybody is cheating and winning high five and/

I'm standing here waving my poetic flag talking about

black pride/

Some days it seems like it died/

Cause on Facebook right now there's/

A little girl twerking/

A homeless man in front of grandma jerking/

Somebody committing suicide who is hurting/

All this in five minutes of surfing/

A wife cheating on her husband with his brother/

A husband shooting up his former workplace because he
was fired for being in the wrong race/

Some bigot yelling at a Islamic temple that he thinks is in
the wrong place/

A Chinese couple beaten over a virus that a government
unleashed on its own face/

Some police officer abusing his power along with his baton
and mace/

And these words float in the air where they search for a
heart that may care/

Yes, I've been relegated to the slums/

Huddled in mass with men and women labeled bums/

Hung from a tree politely from a city that might be in the land of the free/

If I could touch the ground I would take a knee/

Because I was never blue, white or red enough like the president to be all that I could - BE!

PART VIII -

Limit

LIMIT

You see mama my dreams were BIG/

Never ran, never hid/

Breaking generational curses was my bid/

The bridge is broken and all I had was a token/

Took the A train to 34th Street/

Suit and tie, Tim's on my feet/

I forged my lyrical genius in Brooklyn's Bed-Sty/

Fulton Street and Marcy/

Restoration plaza dreaming of pushing a Mazda/

Old boys high found a young poet to lay the force on/

Straight A student and a life in the streets started to fade/

My cut made the grade/

The demons I slayed stayed attached to my memory/

I just kept on pressing on/

Through the storms and the trials/

I put my section of Crown Heights on my back/

As I thumbed through the autobiography of Malcolm X/

I knew they lied on my history/

I knew Huey and King would give me fire and desire/

I filtered each verse with a burst of knowledge, wisdom and
understanding/

Knowing my cypher was 360/

My razor blade filled me with security.

Those bullets fly with no warning.

Those vampires strike when the moon is alit/

And innocent throats are slit in the darkness of New York
alleyways/

Nowadays the strays are not flesh/

They scatter the city from fools with no aim/

We climb the mountain with a whole hood trying to bring us down/

Though you can't blame them/

No one wants to be left/

So, we hold on not knowing some of us do pull ups and push-ups/

And you will never know if you keep holding the stars down/

Let them fly, let them put on that crown/

What goes around comes around/

Success has no out of bounds/

Oohs and aahs are the sounds/

The hounds of hell are biting at our heels/

Just try to avoid the peels/

Only time heals/

We have missed enough meals/

Wheels up in the air/

The only thing we hear is the choir sing there is no –

LIMIT!

/

WILL SEE (*ISAAC BONNER SR.*)

A wise man told me "Longevity Ends"/

And I have thought about it every day/

Wasted seconds, minutes, hours, days, months and years

trying to make the past pay/

She never does/

She is just a trifling bitch that never changes/

And revenge is a waste but the taste is addictive/

I could have just tried to live/

But I died with each attempt to kill something everlasting/

The casting of each spell unlocked a new hell where I

tripped, stumbled and ultimately fell/

Headfirst in the gallows/

The drowning of Eric in a river shallow/

The battle took its toll/

In a forty-year old hole I opened my eyes and saw pestilence run free/

A country fallen over a knee taken for those killed for just being brown/

A sneeze over a town and a cough polluting the air uncovering revelations/

The horsemen stood idle/

My hand clutching a dirty bible/

Knowing that my survival mattered and in the end, nothing else mattered/

Not how rich or poor/

Not the color of your skin/

Not what sexual preference you prefer to engage in/

Not the homeless or the home owner/

Not the pimp or the ho/

Not the dumb or the ones who really know/

Not the president, senator, governor or mayor/

Not the coach or the player/

Not the cool kid or the one being bullied/

Death held no favorites/

Not the poet or the scholar/

Not the victim or the assailant/

Not the vengeful or the perpetrator/

There was no later, only now/

What are we going to do with a world on the brink of
destruction?/

Neither democrat or republican can stop the omega/

My ancestors once said that the stars tell stories of what
was and will be/

I know that I don't have the answers, but brother we all -

WILL SEE

STORY

Out of my cocoon I sprung from a place where Love knew
few/

We were the color blues/

Watched mom trade food stamps for school shoes/

Rolled in crews because we were all hurting/

In the darkness searching for a lighthouse to guide us/

For some light we prayed God would guide us/

My scriptures were built in a music class in which I became
the outcast/

Fate made me play a pen and pad/

When those two closest fell they were all I had/

Writing under candle light another night pops couldn't pay
the bill/

Using a hot plate to eat, yeah it was that real/

Used to the struggle/

Odd jobs like a clown I used to juggle/

Those girls don't love you when you are not hustling/

On the top of my building screaming for freedom and justice/

I noticed America didn't see me/

She didn't see me begging to be free/

I hoped for change/

Still praying for change/

The dream that King dreamed became strange/

In the middle of Sodam and Gomorrah I clutch my Torah/

Looking for a quarter inch of glory/

All I have for the people is my truth and my - STORY!

GODS PLAN

Maybe, just maybe they thought they would feel better about themselves if they called you names/

Maybe their mind games could plot defeat/

Nah, maybe your failure could lead to their success/

Maybe their mental deficiencies will stop God from blessing you/

So, they label you whatever is in the air/

And it hurts because you expect them to carry you when the soul gets weak/

But only God will understand your pain/

So yeah, we put too much faith in man/

Cause we are all flawed/

Broken whether rich or poor/

And you're sitting there wondering why a rich man blows his brains all over the canvas/

It's easier for a camel to go through the eye of a needle/

People will fail you/

People will curse you/

You have to understand this walk is not mines/

It's yours/

There is no applause/

There is no like button to send you peace/

There is no follow button to for a house to lease/

There is no follow button to make your pain cease /

There is no make up for a lost soul/

You have to find joy with your maker/

Who cares what name you give him?/

When millions of us are walking around here without a real last name/

The devil will try to deceive you/

And line up people to see you through the wrong doors /

You can't buy salvation in any stores/

Probably the only way is to close your eyes while your knees hit the floors/

And pray for knowledge, peace and understanding/

You poor unfortunate soul/

You seek control when all we have ever been is Gods controller/

You have to let go of the rein and the pain/

You have to let go of addictive habits like cocaine/

Numbing devices that aid your fall/

Get up brother and sister and answer the only call that matters – GODS!

BRIGHTLY

The moon illuminates the darkness/

The kiss upon my lips soft yet subtle/

The oils massaged in tenderly/

A volcano still in the twilight/

An explosion of passion glazes the sheets/

The beating of the heart sped up by fingertips/

The motion slow yet steady/

The soul left drifting in the air/

Lost in a place where ecstasy slides underneath moans of
pleasure/

Where the tongue gets hidden in places where the hands are
lost/

Trying to taste the essence contained in you/

And the cost is too much to bare/

Where the throbbing subsides with unbridled sensitivity/

And the breathing is strained/

The skin is stained with passion/

Where each crevice is explored and defeated/

The kisses seated with intent to destroy/

The shaking of legs and the search to be held/

While the world stops on a dime/

The moist remains of treasure tasted lovingly/

The darkness of life lifted if only for a moment/

The light shines on sweaty sheets/

And the moon shines this night - BRIGHTLY!

MASTER

I'm not perfect/

Though I have tried to be/

And failed miserably/

Aimed to be the hoods hope/

But the pain of carrying everyone makes it hard to cope/

Makes my dreams and my aspirations collages of mirages/

Switchblade tucked in my sleeve/

This close to making an atheist believe/

 In the dungeon of Hell's Kitchen/

 Pitching lines of my life served as an entree/

My old homie Andre from saint marks keeping tabs on the

on the souls my pen grabs/

 I'm here in the reservoir of humanity's poor/

Living in the middle of death by pearl grip hollow tip, blue

Crip/

My hieroglyphics are depicted on the desk of MS 390/

Clouds in the sky/

Gentrification was the pill that made the hood die/

Lost in the pile was the style of a people who struggled

since they were enchained/

Now we chained ourselves to the vision of their wealth/

We made those colors cross and boss a boss/

Now we stand chained to a ugly 700 dollar purse - at a loss

for words/

Slavery redefined/

And your dollar worth means nothing on this earth/

Especially when the skies open up and destroy every

earthly possession/

Then you will find out you're just a lost slave with no -

MASTER!

THERE

My vernacular borders on the line of spectacular/

But the rapture is near/

I know not how to walk in fear/

Too many masters of ceremony adapting to mumbling

clear/

Strange black fruit still swinging in the southern breeze/

My enemies stand guard over my miscues/

Not many clues to my blues/

My broken heart was on the news/

Heart damaged beyond the physical I still have the bruise/

I got here on a rickety ship it was no cruise/

Love has been the poison of my youth/

The pain gained became the wisdom of my tooth/

My lies and my truth/

February 14th has been the scourge of my existence/

The plight of my existence has been relentless strain/

I wonder if this mess of me can claim victory/

My time here is a mystery/

Visually I'm impaired by a history of violence/

I travel in silence to the guillotine/

Repenting my sins before the mean, cruel and wicked/

My soul and heart has long been evicted/

My pain is depicted on gallery walls/

Studied by masses in literary classes/

Dissected by environmental scientist on tables of

discovery/

Talked about lovingly by those who knew me/

God works his magic through me/

Death is an adversary who booed me/

But truly we've held hands before/

On a floor where my mother lay/

While in my adolescence of dancing to kid and play/

Kind of odd that I never danced that way again/

The death of friends by the same streets I claimed as a base

I thought I couldn't get tagged on/

Thought I was safe til the police yelled freeze/

Geez Louise one sneeze and my spirit is in the breeze/

Sheets wrapped over my shell and all that was seen was my

wallabies/

I'm looking for Eric Christopher Bonner in a zone

decimated by loss/

On the same streets where we used to toss footballs to and

fro'/

I find myself wrapped in grief/

Utter disbelief that I waited too long like Puerto Rico after

a hurricane for relief/

My belief in God keeps the focus clear/

As long as I'm here no matter how difficult the trek for my

people is, I'm going to be - THERE!

TRY

They will break your heart in an attempt to break your mind/

They will break your joy and expect you to be kind/

They will stab you in the back and hope you never look behind/

They will shatter your dreams to see if you still have nightmares/

They will steal your air but expect you not to yell; I can't breathe/

They will kill your love and expect you not to grieve/

They will mock your imagination and get mad when you believe/

They will flog you in a public square and expect you to thank them for the meal/

They will shoot and kill your brother and then tell you at least you have another/

They will dishonor your mother because you grew to be imperfect/

They will test your resolve because they have never overcome their own childhood trauma/

They will call you names unbecoming of who God shaped you to be and not expect a butt whipping/

They will slap you in the face and look in shock because murder was the case they gave you/

They will belittle your walk with The Lord because they could never could wait for him to catch up/

They will not see your growth because you grew where the light could not reach you/

That I walked to my demise eyes on a prize that a boy from the bottom should have never even gazed upon/

And even if I don't win "there is joy in the struggle and ugliness in the success"/

Hope you listen to your heart and not "they" who hate to see you win because in this game called life/

Pain and heartache are a guarantee/

Love is a dream that becomes fool's folly/

And we are all going to die, so let the haters hate and you, you just – TRY!

PART IX -

Philosophy

Philosophy

I wanted my song to be bright/

Alas, I was bred in the pit where you do wrong to make right/

Where you walk in the darkness because the light losses sight/

The threat of death is just a word/

We drink our worries away/

Live for the moment and hope for the day/

We cry, laugh, hurt and live/

We give time for money/

Pray though the bad weather/

Hop-scotch over the sad ones/

Sip a quarter water to quench our thirst/

Dream about being the first to escape/

My story is wrapped in suffering/

But God held me up to glow/

When my friends crucified Eric/

The Truth had to grow/

Under scrutiny and pain/

Love and rain/

Hurt and redemption/

Alone on the mountaintop/

Pen and pad in hand/

Writing the lines to my - PHILOSOPHY!

WE SEE YOU

Hannah Baker I can see your 13 reasons why/

So many lost and I know why/

It's us, we killed you/

Just to fill you/

Your innocence taken away so when you look in the mirror you are no longer still you/

They call you a crazy bitch but you didn't start that way did you?/

I bet most of you didn't think your beauty would make you a target/

To the point most girls turn to being numb, figure you'd make a profit/

Twerk on the gram/

Put a price on each thrust or slam/

Forget it in the club with your girls mixing Hennessy and gin/

Wake up and do the same thing again/

That pain is still there though, it does not disappear/

It never floats away in the air/

Even after marriage you carry it - everywhere/

I see it/

I see it under the make-up and weaves/

The red bottoms and Gucci sleeves/

Looking for superman Like Lois did Christopher Reeves/

Looking for peace like the wind blows leaves/

The assaulted heart grieves/

A soft kiss under the moonlight relieves/

You're more than a number on a list/

The strength of a woman is grand when your house is

broken into and the essence taken; yet you stand/

Only a male inmate on Rikers could understand/

Yet we see it and believe it to be ok or normal/

To all those hiding in the bosom of a shirt too tight, you are

more than that/

More than the shake of a derriere/

How many of you cry in the darkness?/

How many of you put on a mask just to bask in your

glory?/

How many of you are trying to raise men from boys?/

And we become the enemy of the state; all of us combined

with one phallus/

That's what you tell us/

But we failed you and us/

You see us in the darkness salivating over just the touch of your skin/

How many women date women just because they relate to that pain?/

That notion that all we want is your bodies intertwined/

But there are those of us who see your mind and soul before we fall in the hole of ecstasy/

Yet none of us stand up and say be true/

Be different from what the masses do/

Ladies I just wanted you to know I'm telling the world:

When your fully clothed and not dolled up; most of us grown men cherish and guess what/

WE SEE YOU!

I Had To

Peace King/

Still holding on to my peace ring/

Barrels at my head, hands raised/

Wondering if my life even matters to us/

Wondering if all the pain was a must/

Whether we live or die/

Dust to dust/

The wind gust I can't trust/

She might blow uncertainty and change/

The feeling is strange/

Something my pale brother can't comprehend/

My broken heart on the mend eternally/

Under the microscope of my faith/

Knowing that sin begins within/

"Yea though I walk through the valley of death"/

I fear no evil but when the people sworn to protect/

Are the ones I'm most fearful of/

Obsidian gems living, breathing and dying by metal shot with the intent to subdue/

Death becomes true/

As much as the oceans are blue/

My lynching was overdue/

We hold these truths to be self-evident over you/

The guillotine was a dream compared to my nightmares/

In utter lonely darkness I grew amongst the shadows of fluttering street lights/

While Al Green sung background to the sound of my madness/

Facts is I survived a war where all the guns were trained on me/

I had to out-think every rival, the victory was my survival/

Outlined my revival on stages where poetry bloomed/

My spirit doomed to battle/

I tested the snakes rattle/

Rounded up my dreams like cattle/

When they ask me why I spread my wings to fly even though the weather was relentless/

Just tell them – I HAD TO!

Fooled

Black mac, black nine/

Black man on a land mine/

Black jealousy on top of the revelry/

Black Jesus telling me, just pray/

Black cops are going to stop the white ones one day/

Black momma on her knees on a Sunday/

Black computer lens on record for only fans/

Black husband slaving away nine to five/

Black Monday and his own brother in his bed/

Black bullet didn't stop just passed go and went straight in his head/

Black news reports it as just black on black crime/

Black truth is much deeper/

Black sawed off and street sweeper/

Black pride on a red bandanna/

Black eyes under a blue rag/

Black rage now innocent toes get to play freeze tag/

Black bag full of money taken out of the bank/

Black nickel plate that has been starving, one shot point blank/

Black family finally has Thanksgiving dinner/

Black justice is no justice/

Black boy watching momma shoot up/

Black heartbroken now the automatic burst/

Black men lined up in the hearse/

Black women achievements stand tall when the man has a black eye/

Black millionaire on a red eye travelling to Bed-Sty/

Black hand out to a up and coming stand out/

Back scam on a young star all for the clout/

Black scoreboard lit up the rout/

Black fist in the air for the winner of the bout/

Black glass full of stout/

Black souls on ice/

Black dots on the dice/

Black ground saw that four, five and six twice in a row/

Black calico, black shell and no bail/

Black hell but they shout, you are free/

Black anger on my knife/

Black boys still hanging from trees/

Black bodies still float in the seven seas/

Black babies blood drunk in the foreign breeze/

Black strength murdered by Black pharaohs/

Black man with a staff parting the red sea/

Black man with dreads cutting his hair, now Delilah runs free/

Black Judas still stabbing backs/

Black dreams dying over black nightmares/

Black boys injected by Miss Evers/

Black men murdered in their beds is nothing new/

Black lives mattered when the Atlas was Moor/

Black loves mattered when we ruled/

Black people we have been bamboozled to think God is not watching us; we have been – FOOLED!

Lit

Blood splatter on the pavement/

My heart shattered into fragments/

The words jumble together/

The weather report came into my life later than needed/

The pain was already suffered/

Those wounds healed but the scars remain/

Covid-19 came and nothing ever again was the same/

The air alone couldn't be trusted/

The winds of change can't be adjusted/

The touch of love feels like a chokehold/

Our souls dancing in the moonlight/

My lyrics a soft pillow for those hurt like me to lay on/

God bestowed on me the canvas I spray on/

A memory of a distant kiss entraps me/

The skies open lovingly/

Visions of ghosts who whispered they love me – hug me/

I wanted to shine in the dark sky/

A reason for the downtrodden to never give up/

A reason to never quit when the world on your head takes a

shit/

A reason for your light to never dim; but always stay –

LIT!

Succeeded

The clouds spelled out king/

No kingdom meant for me to rule/

Death burned at the stake/

The devil plotted a time and place where The Truth and

The Legend could break/

But, God saved me in a place where the lights never shined

and sets on dreams/

Where stars fall only to die/

Where talent is formed in the abyss of Brooklyn/

Where the gun shots sing a lullaby/

Fast cars and fast women hover by/

We get rich or die trying/

There is no in between/

There is no middle man in life/

When you are formed from the bottom/

We hold on to hope/

Hold on to The Lords hand trying to cope being stuck in the matrix/

To the faces in the crowd always pay the proper homage/

So many people lifted your favorite star before their little lights began to shine/

Every line scribbled I took my time with/

The gift was given to me because I draw with my aorta/

With the passion of Naruto Uzimaki probably/

I didn't let my circumstances hobble me/

I didn't let the ghost trip me when they follow me/

Every poem is toasted with wine/

For the good and bad times/

Both were needed to gauge if we completed the mission

and – SUCCEEDED!

Giving

Is it just poetry under the stars?/

Are the bars just figments of my imagination?/

Are we all on the same trip to our final destination?/

Is the rhythm to my blues too complicated?/

On the backs of the dead each line is dedicated/

On the wishes of a ghetto kid from 390 they find me/

Oh no girl, don't mind me/

I used to walk these streets blindly with a razor waiting for the devil to find me/

That's word to my fallen brother from a Latin mother/

Never one to hide my emotion, there is no cover/

Too much anger; but I paint over it with foolery/

Maybe I joked around too much when I yearned for a pistol to clutch/

Forgive me, my heart is still vengeful/

Can't fight lies spread diligently/

I don't think you'll understand this until God calls this son home/

But I lived through enough sorrow that when I blink I can see the past like ghosts from a crash/

Speaking to me through the musical beats in my ear/

Its supernatural I fear/

As a little one I envisioned the death that came/

I saw each betrayal before it happened, kind of a reason why I never was a ho like Jerry though/

I hear these verses on the wings of a Pegasus/

In the mirror of Medusa I stand frozen/

So, in the shadow of my heart lays darkness and I'm afraid I dwell among the heartless/

So, when they tell you I stalked my past for an apology/

It's true I needed to know that some of the pain could go away/

Have you ever jumped someone and thought why am I beating this kid?/

Never did a thing to me except look like me/

Why did I shoot when I could have walked away?/

I'm blessed and lucky they say/

But I know my day cometh/

The tides bring in the good, bad and the ugly/

I'm just the residue of North Carolina runaway slaves/

They moved from the back woods to these urban caves/

Where gin and joints are thrown in the air/

And the ashes are everywhere/

This life was never fair/

The Truth of me is I sacrificed me for my seeds to be free/

I sacrificed Eric so they could be great/

I sacrificed The Slope and The Truth so they need a tag/

Never need a reason to brag about a body with a toe tag/

I'm just a roaming ghost among the living/

And just for the chance to give them the freedom I could

never achieve is all the thanks worth – GIVING!

PART X -

Black Zeus

Black Zeus

There is only one Truth, please don't listen to a copy/

Across the stars that illuminate the dreams of orphans/

Lay what some call hope/

Strewn across the debirs of promises told that never turned true/

Out of that despair sparks what some call determination/

Out of the contamination of the worlds evil examination/

Came this sensation to start a inferno amongst heavens tapestry/

In this darkness the minds like me get our Big Bang/

On deaths knee we took the blows/

On the river Phoenix I learned to Stand By Me/

We explode in the milky way amongst the stars burned away/

Filtered by constellations nurtured by Ares/

We soar on a winged ram colliding with every negative ion/

Eliminating depression by raising our levels of serotonin/

Cloning our ascent through the telescope of knowing that it

takes a village to raise a kid/

And some burn the village down to feels its warmth/

To feel something from nothing/

To rise above the torture endured/

With the bag secured/

Trying to float on a melody like Chris Stapleton singing

Tennessee Whiskey/

Closing my eyes to a melody soaring through my soul/

Trying to grasp clean air through lungs that started in a

smoky blues juke joint/

Cards on the table/

Gin shots for a dollar if you are able/

All truth no fable/

The floor vibrating our vert being/

If you have never experienced this, the sight may be
European/

The record spinning on loop on a dusty turntable/

Watching the lines disappear into a black abyss of rhythm
and blues/

God left clues in the deviled eggs/

Dancing with my mothers leg while the floor shook like a
tornado that appeared out of the speaker/

My tears flood the tapestry looking back trying to see my
face on God's rear view/

Looking for her voice in the void of living/

Seeing her birthday on my receipt/

Trying to hit her number hoping to feel her touch/

Awakening amongst the backdrop of Good Times/

And Family Matters/

It's a Different World for us all Martin/

I just want to be Uncle Phil to my Fresh Prince/

God gave me Power to rise like Cosby/

But In Living Color the silhouette of my Video Music Box is painted with Different Strokes?

"What you talking about Willis"/

Life is a thrill that cant be duplicated/

One life and some of you are Living Single ready to mingle/

And I mix my Love and Hip Hop while I sit atop a mountain with my "head in the clouds like" – BLACK ZEUS!

Accapella

I am not perfect/

I trip and fall/

Make a mess of it all/

Disfigure a Picasso/

Draw over a Monet/

All in a feeble attempt to be real and not phony/

The road travelled for me bumpy and stony/

Days and nights spent alone pondering the future though I
was abused by my past/

Misused to the last morsel/

Crumbs in my hair/

Splinters in my chair/

I am seated with no fear/

Just a broken aorta damaged beyond repair/

A repaired hernia cause it was a strain to get you here/

Where you can close your eyes and hear me clearly/

With no distraction or interference/

The tracks I inhabit warns of no clearance/

The blood of my poetry covers the walls/

The tracks of my tears is absorbed in the track ties/

The heat is scolding/

My end unfolding/

My children and wife I'm holding tight/

I am praying to God at night/

To forgive my mistakes trying to make a wish/

I was never taught how to fish/

I just survived on my own desperation/

Even when Edenton welcomed me with no hesitation/

I came to realization/

I am a man with no home/

No beats left in my heart/

So, I sing my sonnets in the rain – ACCAPELLA!

REST

Roses bleeding into the moonlight /

The kiss gentle but oh so right/

The squeeze on me tight and snug/

The temperature rising like the sun in the morning/

The heart melting on the surface of ecstasy/

Never dreamed that heaven would lay next to me/

Chestnut eyes staring into a future uncertain but for the

moment perfect/

The rivers of love and happiness colliding with blood in my

stream/

Waking up like was it all a dream?

It would seem that my Symphony of Night is Simons quest/

A Tsunami from Konami?

The origami of my love spilled over the sea/

Every lyric a testament to a life lived in honor and horror/

The touch of ghost hover above me/

I don't even know if those that love me – love me/

Spin kicking friends and foes like Chun Li/

Hope the Ryu and Ken fireball doesn't stun me/

In a game of spit and spades my shades break/

The heart takes it final beat/

And the spirit can finally take a seat to – REST!

<u>Fail</u>

We twist and turn in the wind/

Find ourselves lost in every bend/

Crash into barriers/

Exploding in lust/

Combining with each dust particle and hidden molecule/

I'm bound to you/

From the follicle of the moment I hollered at you/

Out of that sprang a thousand memories/

That intertwined with the mysteries of the universe/

Trapped in intercourse of our discourse/

Was the force that started Star Wars/

Upon the façade of bodega stores/

Our love sprouted from humble seeds/

Before our money dreamed/

We dined on honey buns and farina/

Before our cruise ship docked in Argentina/

We explored each other like the Nina, Pinta and Santa

Maria/

We dreamed of happier days/

When our youth sprouted simpler ways/

When the days were longer/

And our resolve was stronger/

Before the heartache and deception/

When love was thrown with no interception/

You know this was before doubt crept in/

In your busom I slept in/

We were lost in theses city lights/

While the A train played our lullaby/

Serenading us to heaven and hell/

The American dream swallowing us like Jonah the whale/

The air tasted stale/

Together we stood on the precipice of greatness/

Letting the chips fall where they will/

Knowing that God will decide if we succeed or if we –

FAIL!

War

I lived on the ghettoes edge/

Peeked over the ledge of humanity/

Baptized in the river Jordan like Ronnie from the Chi/

Washed my tears away with Hennesey?

Played spades with the devil hoping he would be friendly/

In my trek for success like Omari in Power/

I wanted to be the hoods flower/

Teaching myself piano when the sun sets/

Letting my blood spill on the sheets/

Drunk on love/

Touched by angel above/

If push comes to shove, I will put a hole in any enemy of a
friend to me/

Throw away the key/

I was born a dead man walking/

The slave chain rattles on my O positive blood/

The mud that I traverse left many men in a hearse/

But I disperse the heavens and hells/

And I walk a line like Johnny Cash in between the lines/

Where gospel connects to Kanye/

I sign my own death and birth certificate/

Just playing my song in A minor/

The black and white keys melting under my fingertips/

I close my eyes and see heaven's gate/

While the symphony of my pain is plain and dear to Hells furnace/

I was the residue of a unwanted Jehovah's Witness/

An unwelcome guest in a kingdom where your grandmother doesn't remember the name her daughter gave you/

In a place so dark you pray Jesus can save you/

So, you use all the tools God gave you while the love withers/

The snake slithers over the maiden's dreams/

And he fornicates with wishes that women lust over/

The picture painted so deep you can't brush over/

I just close my eyes and play the keys God blessed me to play/

While the new world order is already in order/

And the chip is already is already in your hand, just a phone to some/

But it contains the knowledge of the forbidden tree/

Eve dying a ho and Adam is just another man deceived/

But they will make most believe that the men are dogs/

The vanity is widespread/

The dead do tell tales/

The battle has only begun/

We fight to go to sleep only to wake up to another day of –

WAR!

PART X -

You Save Me

Save Me

I was hurt, woodened and near death/

Little of what made me Eric left/

Truth is not far from The Legend/

But my tears overflow my joys/

A mother leaves in 93 right in front of me/

A best friend taken by the streets we both romanced/

A love taken by a chance to dance/

A life on the verge of a shutdown/

A crown placed upon my head in a department store/

Wearing a smile all day even though my skies rained like
an Aprils May/

The light in my hazel eyes dimmed in the gigantic oceans
of my blackness I swim in/

"Did you know that you saved me from the fall"/

Wedding bells and all/

You're the reason the MTA gave me that call when Macy's
had me up against the wall/

Trying to fire me unjustly/

But you decided to trust me when the knife was still in my
back/

Moved in when her weave was still on the track/

Helped me past betrayals past/

I tried to return the favor/

I bought whatever I could/

Sorry you had to carry me, when you married me/

Emotionally still shielded some parts of me/

And it takes strength to stand by when I'm carrying all
these ghosts/

It can take a toll believing in someone who failed to find his own sword in the stone/

"We have been through it all"/

Miscarriages, neonatal and trust issues and all/

Fighting for the love when the field is littered with land mines and all/

"I owe it all to you"/

Beautiful twin sons and a perfect angel daughter/

I wouldn't change a quarter/

Even when the court was out of order/

I was bleeding, hit with mortar/

Thank God and I love you – T/

Cause you managed to – SAVE ME!

Wishing on A Star

I wish upon a star/

Just a wish that my kids don't walk through life like this/

Trying to spread your wings only to find out that God never intended for you to soar/

Just to get hurt as a sign that we all can overcome/

Some days I wish that it was me instead of Jim/

Going to the Chinese restaurant with my sister/

A bullet with the name tearing through my neck/

Taking my last breath on the cold January ground/

Uttering a lie that it's OK though/

But it never will/

Forty years old and the 15-year old me still cries when the skies darken/

I wish upon a star/

That maybe my skin color didn't matter/

That in a group interview my intellect shines without the stigma/

That my hazel eyes could have seen a world without color when I was small/

Every day I have lifted my voice and sung/

My hopes and dreams hung; strung up near the strange fruit/

All I learned was how to shoot on top of the roof/

Treat my love like trash because I was told my black women don't like nice men/

Be a thug even in a shirt and tie/

Never flinch a inch/

Never show weakness in the face of death/

Let them shoot until there's no breath/

Until there's nothing left/

Don't mind me ya'll, I'm just wishing on a star in the
winter's night/

That I never held you tightly/

That love was simple but it never is/

That we could walk away without looking back/

My tears leave a track in a stack of sorrow/

Trying to save some of my joy so tomorrow I will have
some to borrow/

Forgive me I tried to build a mansion in the south for every
Bonner/

But it's just me sitting on a Brooklyn balcony staring at the
dark night – WISHING ON A STAR!

Maybe

Maybe I lied to you/

Maybe I died 24 or 27 years ago/

Killed by love, brotherhood and kinship/

Maybe The Truth of The Legend is that life takes more

than it gives/

And sometimes the wounds are covered but they never

truly heal/

They never truly will/

Success is no shield/

Underneath the diamonds is the tears in a game of spit/

The sun shines in memory/

Visually the aesthetic of my scars is "unforgettable and

that's what you are"/

Maybe we are all just hurting ourselves and the ones we love more/

Never healing just moving on dealing with each regret with wine and a cigarette/

But am I the only one not self-medicating/

Not hating my past/

But trying to move forward with peace/

While the world is at war/

Only to fall asleep and realize that with this hue/

I am depended upon to be stronger than most/

Even when I am haunted by ghosts/

That kissed me under the moonlight where souls are lost/

And even the waters that baptized me will not bring me solace/

Maybe it's just me/

Maybe I don't trust me/

Maybe I had a vision of love like Mariah/

Maybe the glass broken that cuts the hands in an eyeglass
store hurts more/

Maybe we are all dying inside/

Putting Gucci on the outside to hide us/

Praying to God to provide us relief/

But maybe there is nothing else but darkness; nothing else
and nothing more/

Maybe just – MAYBE!

Lawrence Street

I lived on Lawrence Street/

And on that street the past repeats and cheats/

Stomps on your subconscious with cleats/

The treats were few and hollow/

I seen despair wallow there in glutinous collections of allegories/

Diagonal in the mistreatment with a love I once knew/

A bone to pick with my maker I may have to sue/

Alone in my humble abode with only my pain to brew/

I sat among the shadows dancing hauntingly with each passing car light/

Awakened to paralysis in my slumber/

I saw angels, demons and in the middle my own mother/

The dead I am afraid they danced in my bed/

The wounds suffered deeply/

I prayed to God to keep me while I cut my wrist/

I popped each prescription pill with the intent to feel comfort and no pain/

Even though I was healed from surgery/

It was just a feeble attempt to murder me/

To go in and steal my life away, just a simple burglary/

And I danced in the glow of knowing for a moment, peace/

Peace on Lawrence Street where dreams wither and we yearn to be an army of one/

Blamed for the injustices I never committed falsely and abundantly/

You see I chiseled out this image of me in the lowest dwellings of humankind/

Blessed with a heart and a beautiful mind/

To death I was never blind/

For she reached out her hands to me while my great

grandmother Ethel Carmichael lay in her coffin when I was

only 5/

But since that trip my eyes saw the void/

I felt the touch intimately under the cover of night/

I saw betrayal lay its hand on hearts and squeeze tightly/

So please sympathize with me when you see me in prayer

with my headphones on/

Don't disturb the walk/

In those headsets the past can talk/

And you can be all you be dreaming on – LAWRENCE

STREET!

CHRISTMAS SOULS

It was important for me to end this/

The sorrow and the joy/

The laughter and the cries/

The pain and the happiness/

My sun and my moon setting on a Christmas noon/

Where all my good memories lie/

Where my grand-mother Annie Bonner would die/

Where a new Nintendo would get unboxed/

Where a friend named Jimmy would become my brother/

Where I can see the last images of my mother/

Where the soft kisses of a lover would forge love where only pain resided/

Where Christmas lights entranced the soul to travel to world where the only song was Silent Night/

And the temptation was to be happy and find it in your own children eyes/

Where you would you be given twin gifts that conquered death/

Where you are forever in debt to the NYU NICU/

Where families join and tether through storms and break ups over stories told that had to be/

No legend but the tale was written by me but shaped by God/

I just performed my best with a hole in my chest/

While the snow falls over a fallen city/

And the past is buried deeply/

Where angels dance in the moonlight/

And miracles occur on the polar express/

I find a little me home alone on a Christmas vacation/

Awakened after my nightmare before Christmas where I die hard/

Trying not to be scrooged by my own Christmas carol/

Visited by three ghosts all with different hosts/

Where G.I. Joe dances with Barbie/

Oddly Santa Clause can't prepare some/

They never fill the thrill/

The gifts are imaginary, never real/

Just wishes of the poor/

In a world where the rich throw money at a stripper/

The disconnect is perilous/

It is a sad display and I fear for not just us but our –

SOULS CHRISTMAS!

SUNSETS

This I am afraid is my last will and testament/

The proceeds of my creativity goes to my seeds for future longevity/

Hold all that revelry and the wishful optimistic dreams you all hold for me/

Rain falls freely/

We all want to be more/

We want our dreams to collide with reality/

When nightmares walk around real-life Elm street more/

The closest to your heart will be the ones who tear you apart/

They will call you a liar to deny the truth/

They will call you delusional when your heart holds all the proof/

The rivers in life will crash into the sea/

The sediment buried under the sand/

The wishes are made on stars fallen/

The ones who do you wrong avoid you/

Yet even Medusa turned to stone when faced with a mirror/

The pen writes a path /

I hid all this pain with my laugh /

We walk towards glory willfully so our enemies can watch our last dance/

Just a last chance to hit the number/

12 disciples pray over our slumber/

The devil walks freely/

Soiling the earth with every step/

The rosary hung tightly/

The prayers are whispered nightly over regrets and secrets/

The innocent suffers in a war zone/

The bullets tear into flesh/

The blood spills in the streets.

And sometimes, sometimes flowers grow/

They bloom in the hands of death and destruction/

In the middle of sensual seduction/

Betrayals force angers hands/

The heart and soul of humanity collapse in revenge/

The fires singe our faith/

The Christmas spirit hovers over our smile/

Basking in the light of joy/

We have stumbled/

We have fallen/

We may or may not rise/

But we shall never yield/

We will never give up/

We will live in the sunrise/

And dance among the stars when the – SUNSETS!

Acknowledgments

I acknowledge everyone and no one. To the ones

who tried to hurt me and to the ones who

abandoned me when I needed you – Thank you. I

used the pain to gain.

I grew where few do.

And though I needed some of you.

I needed me more.

I needed to stand for me.

I needed to stand for Eric In The Shadow of The

Truths Heart.

Goodbye with Love and Peace.

Special shout out to Christ Fellowship Baptist Church in Bed-Sty along with pastor David Kelley.

My Love to Lateva, Aria, Christopher, Christian, Joe and Joann Bonner. Shout out to those who supported my poetry like Kevin, Eatha, Susan, Anthony and Rodney Williams. High five to Lois and Monique Green, Fist Bump to my MTA family Maia, Vikki, Rae, Kerrianne, Robert, Val, Mike, Gaspare, Elton, Vonetta, Kim, Joan, John, Lisa and Rene.